endorsed for
BTEC

CW00495931

REVISE BTEC NATIONAL

Information Technology

REVISION WORKBOOK

Series Consultant: Harry Smith

Authors: Alan Jarvis and Daniel Richardson

A note from the publisher

In order to ensure that this resource offers high-quality support for the associated Pearson qualification, it has been through a review process by the awarding body. This process confirms that this resource fully covers the teaching and learning content of the specification or part of a specification at which it is aimed. It also confirms that it demonstrates an appropriate balance between the development of subject skills, knowledge and understanding, in addition to preparation for assessment.

Endorsement does not cover any guidance on assessment activities or processes (e.g. practice questions or advice on how to answer assessment questions), included in the resource nor does it prescribe any particular approach to the teaching or delivery of a related course.

While the publishers have made every attempt to ensure that advice on the qualification and its assessment is accurate, the official specification and associated assessment guidance materials are the only authoritative source of information and should always be referred to for definitive guidance.

Pearson examiners have not contributed to any sections in this resource relevant to examination papers for which they had prior responsibility.

Examiners will not use endorsed resources as a source of material for any assessment set by Pearson.

Endorsement of a resource does not mean that the resource is required to achieve this Pearson qualification, nor does it mean that it is the only suitable material available to support the qualification, and any resource lists produced by the awarding body shall include this and other appropriate resources.

Pearson

Published by Pearson Education Limited, 80 Strand, London, WC2R 0RL.

www.pearsonschoolsandfecolleges.co.uk

Copies of official specifications for all Edexcel qualifications may be found on the website: www.edexcel.com

Typeset and illustrated by Kamae Design, Oxford
Produced by Out of House Publishing
Cover illustration by Miriam Sturdee

First published 2017

20 19 18 17
10 9 8 7 6 5 4 3 2 1

British Library Cataloguing in Publication Data
A catalogue record for this book is available from the British Library

ISBN 978 1 292 15035 2

Printed in Slovakia by Neografia

Acknowledgements
We are grateful to the following for permission to reproduce copyright material:

Screenshots:
Microsoft product screenshot(s) reprinted with permission from Microsoft Corporation on pages 45–46, pages 90–92, pages 99–104, pages 106–108.

A note from the publisher
In order to ensure that this resource offers high-quality support for the associated Pearson qualification, it has been through a review process by the awarding body. This process confirms that this resource fully covers the teaching and learning content of the specification or part of a specification at which it is aimed. It also confirms that it demonstrates an appropriate balance between the development of subject skills, knowledge and understanding, in addition to preparation for assessment.

Endorsement does not cover any guidance on assessment activities or processes (e.g. practice questions or advice on how to answer assessment questions), included in the resource nor does it prescribe any particular approach to the teaching or delivery of a related course.

While the publishers have made every attempt to ensure that advice on the qualification and its assessment is accurate, the official specification and associated assessment guidance materials are the only authoritative source of information and should always be referred to for definitive guidance.

Pearson examiners have not contributed to any sections in this resource relevant to examination papers for which they have responsibility.

Examiners will not use endorsed resources as a source of material for any assessment set by Pearson.

Endorsement of a resource does not mean that the resource is required to achieve this Pearson qualification, nor does it mean that it is the only suitable material available to support the qualification, and any resource lists produced by the awarding body shall include this and other appropriate resources.

Introduction

This Workbook has been designed to support you in preparing for the externally assessed units of your course. Remember that you won't necessarily be studying all the units included here – it will depend on the qualification you are taking.

BTEC National Qualification	Externally assessed units
Certificate	2 Creating Systems to Manage Information
Extended Certificate and Foundation Diploma	1 Information Technology Systems 2 Creating Systems to Manage Information

Your Workbook

Each unit in this Workbook contains either one or two sets of revision questions or revision tasks, similar to those you will be set for your actual assessment. Working through these will help you to become familiar with the way in which you will be assessed and to develop the skills you require.

This Workbook will often include one or more useful features that explain or break down longer questions or tasks. Remember that these features won't appear in your actual assessment!

Grey boxes like this contain **hints and tips** about how to complete a task, interpret a brief, understand a concept or structure your responses.

Guided

This icon will appear next to a **partial sample answer** to a question or task outcome. You should read the partial answer carefully, then complete it in your own words.

This is a revision activity. It won't be one of the outcomes you need to produce in your actual assessment, but it will help you understand the processes you will need to go through.

Links

These boxes will tell you where you can find more help in Pearson's BTEC National Revision Guide. Visit **www.pearsonschools.co.uk/revise** for more information.

There is often space on the pages for you to write in. However, if you are carrying out research and making ongoing notes, you may want to use separate paper. Similarly, some units will be assessed through submission of digital files, or on screen, rather than on paper. Make sure you read the guidance for each unit that is given to you by Pearson and your teacher.

Contents

Revision Guide also available for externally assessed units ISBN 9781292150369

A small bit of small print

Pearson publishes Sample Assessment Material and the Specification on its website. This is the official content and this book should be used in conjunction with it. The questions in this book have been written to help you practise the knowledge and skills you will require for your assessment. Remember: the real assessment may not look like this.

Unit 1: Information Technology Systems

Your exam

You will have 2 hours to complete your Unit 1 exam paper. You need to answer every question in the spaces provided. The paper is worth **90 marks** in total. The maximum number of marks available for each question indicates the amount of time you should spend on that question. The amount of writing or drawing space available will also give you an idea of how much detail is needed in each of your answers. There may be more space than you need – you do not have to fill in all the space.

When in your exam:
- use correct spelling, punctuation and grammar, and use appropriate technical language in your answers
- use a pen that writes in black and make sure you also have a spare one with you
- ensure you attempt all questions.

Your exam questions

The exam is composed of several written questions.
- **Each question** is divided into several parts, for example a, b, c.
- **The marks** for each question part are shown in a grey box.
- You will be assessed on your **understanding of computer systems** and the **implications of their use in personal and professional situations**.
- **The questions** will relate to content areas in the specification:
  - digital devices in IT systems
  - transmitting data
  - operating online
  - protecting data and information
  - impact of IT systems on individuals and organisations
  - issues resulting from the use of IT systems.

Each question starts with a **case study**.
- The case study relates to an **individual or organisation**.
- As you work through the parts of the question you will be given **different information** about the person or organisation.
- The parts of the questions will relate to the **different information** you are given.
- Make sure you **focus your answers** on the **needs of the individual or organisation** described in the case study.

You will be asked questions from these **types of questions**. This workbook provides guidance on many of these question types:

Analyse Assess Calculate Complete Demonstrate Describe Discuss Draw
Explain Evaluate Identify Produce State, name, give Write.

Links To help you revise for your Unit 1 exam this workbook contains two full sets of revision questions starting on pages 2 and 13. See the introduction on page iii for more information on features included to help you revise.

Revision test 1

Guided

1 Excelsior IT Support are a contract IT support company. Their employees need to travel to different offices regularly in order to complete repairs and they often do not return to Excelsior IT Support's head office all day. When the technicians take on a job they need to:

- look up the location of the company they need to visit
- look up the details of the problem
- update the status of the job once the visit has been completed.

(a) Explain two features of mobile devices that would make them suitable for use by Excelsior IT Support's technicians for tracking their jobs.

4 marks

There are two marks available for each feature. The first mark is for identifying the feature and the second is for an appropriate expansion, in this case explaining why that feature would be useful for Excelsior IT Support. The features have been given in these example answers – you need to add the expansion for each.

1 Mobile devices like smartphones and tablets can use mobile internet connections, which ....

....

....

2 Mobile devices are also extremely portable, which ....

....

....

....

Links Revise the features of different digital devices by looking at pages 1 and 2 of Unit 1 in the Revision Guide.

(b) Excelsior IT Support has also considered investing in personal laptop computers for their technicians as an alternative to mobile devices.

Discuss the features of laptops that might make them more suitable for the technicians.

The question asks you to "Discuss the features of laptops....". This discussion requires you to identify a good range of features and give appropriate reasons for their importance, in the context of the question.

6 marks

1 Laptops are portable computing devices which ....

....

....

....

....

....

....

....

2 A laptop has a separate keyboard, as well as a large screen and a touchpad. These ....

(c) In order for the IT technicians to access and update customer information on their mobile devices, this information needs to be transmitted over the internet.

The management at Excelsior IT Support are concerned about the legal and ethical issues of transmitting personal data, such as customers' names and addresses, and storing them on the portable devices.

> You can discuss a range of factors here. Laws such as the Data Protection Act and the Computer Misuse Act clearly apply, as do moral and ethical issues such as customer privacy and protection of data.
> As this is an evaluation question, make sure you look at both the positive and negative issues and the extent of their impact on Excelsior IT Support.

Evaluate the impact on Excelsior IT Support of the legal, moral and ethical issues that relate to the use of this data in this way. **12 marks**

The Data Protection Act is a piece of legislation that requires businesses like Excelsior to ensure that personal information is kept secure. If Excelsior is found to be not protecting the data being stored and transmitted sufficiently, then the company could potentially face penalties of hundreds of thousands of pounds. In order to comply with the Data Protection Act, Excelsior need to implement security measures, including technology, training and procedures, which could be very costly.

However, a positive impact of the Data Protection Act is that it increases consumer confidence in supplying their data to a business, which makes it a lot easier for Excelsior to carry out their work.

> Go on to evaluate the Computer Misuse Act, explaining its positive impacts on Excelsior.

Continue by covering Excelsior's moral obligations regarding the transmission and storage of customers' personal information, such as protecting customer privacy and use of personal data only for clearly defined purposes. You might also consider ethical issues, such as the environmental impact of using portable devices.

Make sure you include a conclusion, summing up the extent of the impact of the legal, moral and ethical issues on Excelsior IT.

Links You can revise legal issues on pages 27 and 38 of Unit 1 in the Revision Guide. Look at pages 36 and 37 to revise moral and ethical issues.

Total for Question 1 = 22 marks

Guided

2 A2B Taxis are a small taxi company based in Reading, Berkshire.

In order to expand their business, A2B Taxis are researching new ways of increasing awareness of their business and attracting customers.

They are looking at using IT systems and the internet in order to communicate with customers and raise brand awareness.

They are considering the use of online communities in particular but are unsure about what benefits these will bring them.

They would also like to investigate how they could use technology to:

- help drivers work more efficiently, by navigating and allocating jobs
- assist dispatchers to deploy drivers in an effective manner
- be more accessible to customers.

(a) Describe three ways that A2B Taxis could use online communities in order to communicate with their customers. **6 marks**

There are two marks for each online communication method. You need to identify and describe each method and expand on it by commenting on how it could be used by A2B Taxis to communicate with their customers.

Fill in the gaps in this example answer using these words:
blogs forums social media network up-to-date feedback service advertise

1 .... websites allow businesses to create and share information and to .... One example is the use of business pages, which would allow A2B Taxis to .... deals directly to customers.

2 .... are regularly updated websites that are often used by businesses to share .... news and information. A2B Taxis could use this method to inform customers of improvements and innovations in the .... they offer.

3 .... are online discussion sites which could be used by the business to gain customer .... on their services.

Links You can revise uses of online communities on page 23 of Unit 1 in the Revision Guide.

(b) The management at A2B Taxis have some concerns about the potential negative impact of online communities on their business, but they are also aware of the potential benefits.

Analyse the impact that online communities might have on A2B Taxis. **10 marks**

Break down this question into parts. What will have a positive impact? Why will it have a positive impact? How does that relate to A2B Taxis? Then look at the negative impacts the same way.

One way that online communities might have a positive impact on A2B Taxis is in helping them to understand customer needs. This is achieved as online communities allow ....

Explain how online communities can help A2B Taxis understand their customers' needs. Then go on to discuss two more potentially positive implications for A2B Taxis.

....

....

....

....

....

....

....

....

....

Links You can revise the implications of business uses of online communities on page 24 of Unit 1 in the Revision Guide.

A negative impact on A2B Taxis of using online communities could be the costs involved. Costs are incurred because

> Explain why costs are involved in the use of online communities. Then go on to cover a couple more potentially negative impacts on the business.

....

....

....

....

....

....

....

....

....

....

....

....

....

(c) The management at A2B Taxis have also been considering how they could use digital devices to improve the efficiency of their business.

Discuss how digital devices could improve the efficiency of A2B Taxis. **10 marks**

> You need to consider a range of devices here, not just the most obvious ones (e.g. smartphones). Think about those that will be of most benefit to a taxi company.

In-car navigation systems have become a major part of the service provided by taxi companies like A2B Taxis because ....

....

....

....

....

Mobile devices, specifically smartphones, would be useful to A2B taxis as ...

Personal computers could be used in the offices of A2B Taxis to help them ...

Communication devices used for internet access would also be of benefit for ...

Links You can revise a range of digital devices and their uses on pages 1–3 of Unit 1 in the Revision Guide.

Total for Question 2 = 26 marks

Guided **3** Benjamin runs a small finance company that employs four members of staff, in addition to Benjamin himself.

Each member of staff has their own standalone PC which stores the files they work on locally.

Staff members often need to share documents, which they do either by emailing them using the business's internet connection, or by transferring them using a USB memory stick.

The documents they share often contain sensitive personal and financial information about the customers who invest with them.

(a) Analyse the benefits of using cloud storage facilities for the finance company's staff to share documents. **6 marks**

There are a wide variety of benefits to cloud storage services to choose from. Here are some suggestions. Expand on these points by clearly explaining how these are benefits to Benjamin's finance company.

Cloud storage services would allow the finance company to share access to folders ....

....

....

....

....

Employees could access the files while away from the office computers ....

....

....

....

....

Cloud storage would make it easier for employees to work on the same documents ....

....

....

....

....

Links You can revise cloud storage on pages 21 and 22 of the Revision Guide, Unit 1.

(b) Benjamin has heard that a possible alternative to using cloud computing for sharing files would be a local area network. He has also heard that a LAN has other uses.

Two uses have been identified (see page 9). Finish them by explaining why each use is helpful to Benjamin's business.

Explain two uses, other than sharing files, of using a LAN in Benjamin's business. **4 marks**

Links You can revise security techniques on page 26 of Unit 1 in the Revision Guide.

A local area network can be used to share a printer ....

....

....

....

A local area network can make backing data up more centralised and structured ....

....

....

....

(c) Benjamin is also considering using cloud computing software. However, he is concerned about the potential drawbacks of using these services.

Analyse whether Benjamin should start using cloud computing software in his business. **10 marks**

Make sure you cover both the benefits and drawbacks of cloud computing software (note that you need to address cloud software, not storage). Include a range and make sure you relate each back to the finance company.

Cloud computing software could benefit Benjamin's business as it will help ....

....

....

....

....

....

....

....

Some disadvantages of cloud computing software for Benjamin could be ....

....

....

....

....

....

....

....

Links You can revise cloud computing software on pages 21 and 22 of Unit 1 in the Revision Guide.

Total for Question 3 = 20 marks

Guided

4 Jessica wants to start making a video series in which she will review newly released technology devices. She wants to share her videos online using well-known video sharing websites.

Jessica would like her videos to be in high definition, even though she is aware that sharing large video files online can be difficult as they can take a long time to download.

(a) Explain how bandwidth and latency affect streaming video over the internet. **4 marks**

Complete the definitions of bandwidth and latency, and then complete the explanation of how each of these affects video streaming. Choose from these sentence endings:

a) the time delay for a data packet to transfer to its destination.

b) to transfer the large amounts of data in a high definition video file.

c) to avoid buffering (ensure that video reaches your computer as fast as it is playing).

d) the rate of data transfer over a network.

1 Bandwidth is ....

....

High bandwidth is required ....

....

....

2 Latency is ....

....

Low latency, or lack of latency, is preferred ....

....

....

Links To revise data transmission issues, turn to page 20 of Unit 1 in the Revision Guide.

(b) Jessica knows that the file format used for videos can affect the file size and suitability for sharing online.

Analyse the impact of different file types for streaming video content. **6 marks**

For this question you should look at a couple of different video file formats and explain both the benefits and the drawbacks of that format for Jessica's needs.

One file format that is commonly used for videos is the .avi format. This would potentially be of use to Jessica as ....

....

....

The drawback for Jessica of this file type is ....

....

....

Another file format for videos is the .mp4 format. This would be of use to Jessica as ....

....

....

The drawback for Jessica of using this file type is ....

....

....

Links To revise file formats, look at page 11 of Unit 1 in the Revision Guide.

(c) To further reduce the size of her videos, Jessica is thinking of using compression. However, she is concerned with how this might affect the quality of her videos.

Assess the impact of different compression tools and techniques on the videos. **12 marks**

> The command word here is 'assess'. So for this question you should compare the pros and cons of a range of compression tools and techniques.

Compression is used to reduce the amount of data required to store a file. By compressing the video files Jessica will ....

....

....

....

....

....

....

....

....

There are two types of compression that are used. One is lossy, the other is lossless. Lossy compression is ....

....

....

....

....

....

....

....

....

....

An extremely important tool for compressing video files for transmitting over a network is a codec.

This is used to ....

....

....

....

....

....

....

....

....

....

....

....

....

....

....

....

....

....

....

....

....

....

....

....

....

Links Revise compression issues by turning to pages 11 and 20 of Unit 1 of the Revision Guide.

Total for Question 4 = 22 marks

END OF TEST

TOTAL FOR TEST = 90 MARKS

Revision test 2

1 Lloyd works for a game development company as a game artist. He performs a variety of tasks including:

- creating high-quality 3D models of landscapes and player characters
- creating 2D textures for game models
- user interface design for game menus, etc.

(a) Lloyd needs to save his 2D graphic files in a format that can be used in the games.

Explain two features of the PNG format that would make it appropriate for this use.

You need to identify two features and explain why each feature is useful for Lloyd's game art.

4 marks

1 ....

....

....

2 ....

....

....

....

Links To revise file formats, turn to page 11 of Unit 1 in the Revision Guide.

(b) Lloyd wants to purchase a new PC to produce his artwork as the one he is using is quite old and it is running slowly.

The table shows the specifications of two computers Lloyd is considering.

	Computer 1	**Computer 2**
Processor	2.7 GHz Quad Core	3.5 GHz Dual Core
RAM	8 GB	4 GB
Storage	1 TB Hard Disk Drive	250 GB Solid State Drive
Graphics	4 GB Dedicated Graphics	Integrated Graphics

You can approach this question by looking at each of the categories in turn and comparing which is more suitable. You should provide a recommendation for which system would be better for Lloyd.

Assess the suitability of these two specifications for Lloyd's needs.

8 marks

....

....

....

....

....

....

Links To revise choosing an IT system, turn to page 14 of Unit 1 of the Revision Guide.

(c) Lloyd is thinking of using cloud storage for saving his graphics files.

Discuss the features and implications of using cloud storage for Lloyd.

10 marks

As well as exploring how cloud storage can help Lloyd, you also need to explain ways in which it might be a hindrance. Some things to consider could be sharing files and security issues.

....

....

....

....

....

....

....

....

....

....

....

....

....

Links Revise cloud storage by looking at pages 21–22 of Unit 1 of the Revision Guide.

Total for Question 1 = 22 marks

2 Harold owns a chain of four fast food restaurants.

He employs a manager as well as several till workers at each restaurant.

The manager at each restaurant is responsible for ordering stock, but Harold keeps the accounts for the business himself on his home desktop PC.

To help improve efficiency, Harold is looking into implementing new self-service food ordering EPOS systems.

(a) Describe two input devices that might be used on a self-service EPOS till. **4 marks**

> Think of two different input devices that are commonly used at the checkout in shops. To help you, think back to when you've used a self-service check-out or food ordering point.

1 ....

....

....

....

....

....

....

2 ....

....

....

....

....

....

....

> **Links** You can revise relevant input devices on pages 2 and 4 of Unit 1 of the Revision Guide.

(b) The new self-service EPOS till system requires a menu-based user interface. The first screen of the user interface should allow the customers to:

- choose from a range of food categories
- choose to go to payment.

Draw a suitable user interface for this first screen in the space provided.

Don't just draw a simple menu. Consider prompts to help the user enter the data, and don't forget accessibility requirements. For example, what options could you add to help people with a visual impairment use the interface?

6 marks

Links Revise user interfaces on page 9 of Unit 1 of the Revision Guide.

(c) Harold would like to gather data from customers on whether there is enough interest in adding these new self-service tills.

Discuss the benefits to Harold of using primary data collection over secondary sources.

10 marks

Discuss a range of benefits of primary data collection and compare each of them to secondary sources to show why primary sources are better for Harold's needs. Don't worry about including the benefits of secondary data collection – that's not needed here.

....

....

....

....

....

....

....

....

....

....

....

....

....

....

....

....

....

....

....

....

....

....

....

....

Links You can revise primary data collection on page 32 of Unit 1 in the Revision Guide.

Total for Question 2 = 20 marks

3 Aaliyah is a sales representative for a large multi-national soft drinks company.

She has a desk and computer at the company's head office, but she rarely goes there. She works mainly from home or during train journeys as she travels between stores that stock the company's drinks.

She completes the bulk of her work on her home desktop PC, using spreadsheet software and word processing software.

While travelling, she takes notes by hand which she enters on the desktop PC when she returns home.

(a) Explain two technologies that will help Aaliyah to work remotely but still have access to her desktop applications, and secure access to company documents and systems. **4 marks**

Think about how Aaliyah could access the files and software on the computer at the head office while working from home. Also consider how to ensure data can be transferred securely between her home and the office.

1 ....

....

....

....

2 ....

....

....

....

Links To revise technologies used in remote working, look at page 22 of Unit 1 of the Revision Guide.

(b) Aaliyah has decided that she needs a digital device for working on while she is travelling. She is considering asking the company to buy her a tablet computer.

Discuss the features of a mobile computing device, such as a tablet, that will make it suitable for Aaliyah's needs. **6 marks**

Always refer back to the case study. Remember that Aaliya will be using her mobile computing device to use productivity software while travelling. What makes such a device appropriate for her needs? This question asks you to 'discuss'. You need to begin be explaining a wide range of features, continuing on to consider how they will be suitable for Aaliyah and how she might use the device.

....

....

....

....

....

....

....

....

....

Links To revise mobile devices, see page 1 of Unit 1 of the Revision Guide.

(c) Aaliyah's manager has told her that the company is considering setting up a fan page on social media to promote the company and encourage direct communication, in order to strengthen their brands.

Evaluate the implications that the company needs to consider before setting up a presence on social media.

12 marks

You should consider how the company can be affected in both a positive and negative manner, as well as the more obvious considerations such as cost and security.

Links: Revise cloud storage and computing by looking at pages 21 and 22 of Unit 1 of the Revision Guide.

Total for Question 3 = 22 marks

4 Haldrech Security are a security company that have been providing physical security for businesses for many years.

They are becoming increasingly aware that they need to modernise their security services.

This will include making better use of technology in the security services they already provide, as well as offering security for IT-based threats.

(a) Before they go any further in implementing new technology systems, Haldrech Security's management would like to know more about the ethical issues involved in using technology systems.

You need to identify and describe each of these ethical implications. Make sure you relate each one to Haldrech Security.

Explain three ethical implications of using technology systems. **6 marks**

1 ....

....

....

2 ....

....

....

3 ....

....

....

....

Links You can revise the moral and ethical implications of using IT systems on pages 36 and 37 of Unit 1 of the Revision Guide. Page 37 is particularly relevant here.

(b) Haldrech Technology want to ensure they have all the processes and technologies in place to protect their clients' IT systems from threats.

Explain how different techniques for protecting IT systems and data work. **8 marks**

Here you need to look at relevant IT security techniques (not legislation) and explain how they protect IT systems and the data stored on them from harm.

....

....

....

....

....

....

....

....

....

....

....

....

....

....

....

....

....

....

....

....

....

....

Links You can revise data protection techniques on page 26 of Unit 1 in the Revision Guide.

(c) Haldrech Security want to gain a better understanding of exactly how legislation will help them to prevent the threats that impact on IT systems.

Evaluate the impact of relevant legislation on the use of technology systems for Haldrech Security in their decision to modernise their services.

Here you should cover a range of legislation, look at what threats they protect against and how they protect against these threats (e.g. what the penalties are for people who break these laws).

12 marks

....

....

....

....

....

....

....

....

....

....

....

....

....

....

....

....

....

....

....

Links To revise the legislation, turn to pages 27 and 38 of Unit 1 in the Revision Guide.

Total for Question 4 = 26 marks

END OF TEST

TOTAL FOR TEST = 90 MARKS

Unit 2: Creating Systems to Manage Information

Your set task

You will complete your task on a computer in exam conditions over a period of 10 hours, which will be split over several sessions during one week. The whole task will be worth 66 marks.

You will need to complete six activities during your supervised assessment period.

Activity 1: Entity relationship diagram

Produce an entity relationship diagram (ERD) for the database by normalising the given data to third normal form.

You are advised to spend 1 hour on this activity.

Total for Activity 1 = 8 marks.

Activity 2: Data dictionary

Produce a data dictionary for your database.

You are advised to spend 1 hour on this activity.

Total for Activity 2 = 8 marks.

Activity 3: Design specification

Complete the design specification documents for your database.

Ensure sufficient information is provided for a third party to implement the interface for your solution.

You are advised to spend 1 hour and 45 minutes on this activity.

Total for Activity 3 = 6 marks.

Activity 4: Testing plan

Create a test log to plan how you will test your completed database.

You are advised to spend 1 hour on this activity.

Total for Activity 4 = 6 marks.

Activity 5: Database development and testing

Develop and test your database using the information in the documents you produced for activities 1 to 4.

Record your database development as annotated screenshots in a single document.

Your screenshots should show:

- your tables, including the fields and attributes
- your table relationships
- your queries, including fields and criteria
- the output of your queries
- the forms you have created
- the reports you have created
- evidence of working validation.

You are advised to spend 4 hours on this activity.

Total for Activity 5 = 26 marks.

Activity 6: Evaluation of your database solution

Evaluate your solution.

You should consider:

- how well your solution meets the requirements of the scenario
- the quality, performance and usability of the database
- the changes made during the development and testing process.

You are advised to spend 1 hour on this activity.

Total for Activity 6 = 12 marks.

Links To help you revise for your Unit 2 set task, this workbook contains two full sets of revision activities starting on pages 28 and 63. See the introduction on page iii for more information on features included to help you revise.

Revision task 1

Set task brief

Task scenario

Your supervisor at Harrow Fix-IT, a small IT support company, has asked you to develop a database to record IT customer support requests. The company provides IT support for five customers, which are local small businesses. The company employs four technicians:

Wendy Simpson – Senior Technician, mobile number 07899 22222

Mohammed Ahmed – Technician, mobile number 07877 33333

David Platt – Technician, mobile number 07888 44444

Winston Jamal – Junior Technician, mobile number 07866 55555

The five customers are:

AB Supplies – 55 High Street, Wembley, HA0 9XX

Station Garage – Station Road, Neasden, NW10 8ZZ

Smith Partners – 21 The Avenue, Neasden, NW10 4OO

Western Engineering – Wembley Industrial Estate, Wembley, HA9 7BB

West London Accountants – 34 Main Road, Harrow, HA1 2YY

Always read the bullet points under 'You need to' carefully. They give lots of information about what you need to include in your database.

You need to:

- design a database structure that:
  - includes support request, customer and technician data
  - avoids unnecessary duplication of data
  - validates data input to ensure integrity
  - has a suitable user interface for technicians that enter support requests, and updates support requests with resolution of problems.

1. The first sub-bullet point above gives clues as to which tables you will need in your database.
   - How many tables will you need?

   ....

2. The bullet point above tells you which data entry forms you will need for your database.

   How many data entry forms will you need to create?

   ....

- import and manipulate the given data
- provide database outputs showing:
  - all unresolved requests
  - all unresolved requests for a particular technician
  - a monthly summary report of all requests dealt with by a particular technician
  - a monthly summary report of all requests from a particular customer
  - a report showing the time a particular technician takes to resolve requests.

3. The sub-bullet points at the bottom of page 28 tell you which queries and reports you will need for your database.

   (a) How many queries will you need to create?

   ....

   (b) How many reports will you need to create?

   ....

- test your database, adding data to ensure that the database meets all requirements
- evaluate your database against the given requirements.

Information

Currently your supervisor uses a spreadsheet to record support requests and resolutions. Figure 1 shows an extract of the data.

4. Look at the table in Figure 1 and identify the two sets of repeating data, together with the fields that are associated with them. Use a different colour highlighter for each.

You can download the .csv file containing the data for the Harrow FIX-IT database by scanning this link with your smartphone or tablet. Alternatively, go to the following link: http://activetea.ch/2gNTa18.

Figure 1

Request ID	Customer	Customer address	Reported by	Date/time reported	Problem description	Technician allocated	Technician job title	Technician mobile no.	Resolved?	Date/time resolved	Resolution description
1	AB Supplies	55 High Street, Wembley, HA0 9XX	Hannah McMahon	27/2/16 0945	Mouse does not work	David Platt	Technician	07888 44444	Yes	28/2/16 1430	Replaced mouse
2	Station Garage	Station Road, Neasden, NW10 8ZZ	Kyle Jones	27/2/16 1030	Application error	Winston Jamal	Junior Technician	07866 55555	No		
3	AB Supplies	55 High Street, Wembley, HA0 9XX	Holly Williams	27/2/16 1415	Forgot login password	Mohammed Ahmed	Technician	07877 33333	Yes	28/2/16 1015	Password reset
4	Smith Partners	21 The Avenue, Neasden, NW10 4OO	Aras Kudirka	27/2/16 1610	No internet access	Mohammed Ahmed	Technician	07877 33333	Yes	1/3/16 1100	Reset router
5	Western Engineering	Wembley Industrial Estate, Wembley, HA9 7BB	Mohsin Iqbal	28/2/16 1020	Shared folder not accessible	Wendy Simpson	Senior Technician	07899 22222	Yes	1/3/16 1545	Mapped shared drive
6	West London Accountants	34 Main Road, Harrow, HA1 2YY	Sunita Shah	28/2/16 1115	Emails not sending	David Platt	Technician	07888 44444	No		
7	Smith Partners	21 The Avenue, Neasden, NW10 4OO	James Smith	28/2/16 1430	Website certificate error	David Platt	Technician	07888 44444	Yes	1/3/16 0915	Checked and all OK
8	AB Supplies	55 High Street, Wembley, HA0 9XX	Keith Evans	28/2/16 1545	Cannot print	Winston Jamal	Junior Technician	07866 55555	Yes	2/3/16 1030	Reset printer
9	Western Engineering	Wembley Industrial Estate, Wembley, HA9 7BB	Jack Dyson	1/3/16 1015	Mapped drive error	Wendy Simpson	Senior Technician	07899 22222	No		
10	Smith Partners	21 The Avenue, Neasden, NW10 4OO	Mai Chen	1/3/16 1100	Files missing	Winston Jamal	Junior Technician	07866 55555	No		
11	Smith Partners	21 The Avenue, Neasden, NW10 4OO	Alice Scott	1/3/16 1530	Keyboard characters incorrect	Mohammed Ahmed	Technician	07877 33333	No		
12	Station Garage	Station Road, Neasden, NW10 8ZZ	Olivia Hill	1/3/16 1620	Cannot connect to WiFi	David Platt	Technician	07888 44444	Yes	2/3/16 1415	Reset WiFi access point
13	West London Accountants	34 Main Road, Harrow, HA1 2YY	Amy Sugar	2/3/16 0920	Hard disk full	Mohammed Ahmed	Technician	07877 33333	No		
14	Western Engineering	Wembley Industrial Estate, Wembley, HA9 7BB	Tinashe Deka	2/3/16 1015	Internet very slow	Wendy Simpson	Senior Technician	07899 22222	No		
15	Station Garage	21 The Avenue, Neasden, NW10 4OO	Roger Bradley	2/3/16 1245	Virus alert	Winston Jamal	Junior Technician	07866 55555	No		
16	West London Accountants	34 Main Road, Harrow, HA1 2YY	Nick Lawson	2/3/16 1500	Accidentally deleted files	David Platt	Technician	07888 44444	No		

Activity 1: Entity relationship diagram

Produce an entity relationship diagram (ERD) for the database by normalising the given data to third normal form.

Remember that normalisation avoids **data redundancy** and makes your database more efficient.

Guided

1. Look at the table of data on page 30. Identify two types of repeating data. The first one has been done for you.

   These will be the **tables** which will store one record for each of the repeating items in the data.

   (a) Customer

   (b) ....

2. Write down the **attributes** (fields) which belong to each item of repeating data. The first two have been started for you. You may not need all the boxes.

Customer	
Customer address	

3. Check if all the fields in these two tables are atomic. List any fields which are not atomic, and list the fields they should be split into.

   ....

   ....

4. Identify the **primary key** for each of these tables.

   Remember a 'made up key' is often the best choice for a primary key. You will need to add a field for this.

   Primary key for the Customer table is ....

   Primary key for the .... table is ....

   Links: You can revise primary and foreign keys by looking at page 52 of Unit 2 in the Revision Guide.

5. The remaining data stores information about individual support requests. You can call the table containing this data **Support _request**.

   List the fields for this table from the sample data, and identify the primary key.

Links: Revise the normalisation process by looking at pages 55 and 56 of Unit 2 in the Revision Guide.

6. What type of relationships will exist between the tables?

   (a) The **Customer** table is related to the **Support _request** table by a

   ☐ one-to-one relationship

   ☐ one-to-many relationship

   ☐ many-to-many relationship.

   > Remember that you create the relationship between the tables by taking the primary key from the table at the 'one' end of a relationship and inserting it in the related records at the 'many' end, where it is referred to as a **foreign key**.

   (b) The .... table is related to the **Support _request** table by a

   ☐ one-to-one relationship

   ☐ one-to-many relationship

   ☐ many-to-many relationship.

   > The first two table headings have been included for you. Look at your answer to the guided revision activity above to identify the third table heading.

7. The Support_request table will need two foreign keys.

   What will these be?

   .... and ....

   Complete the entity relationship diagram for your database.

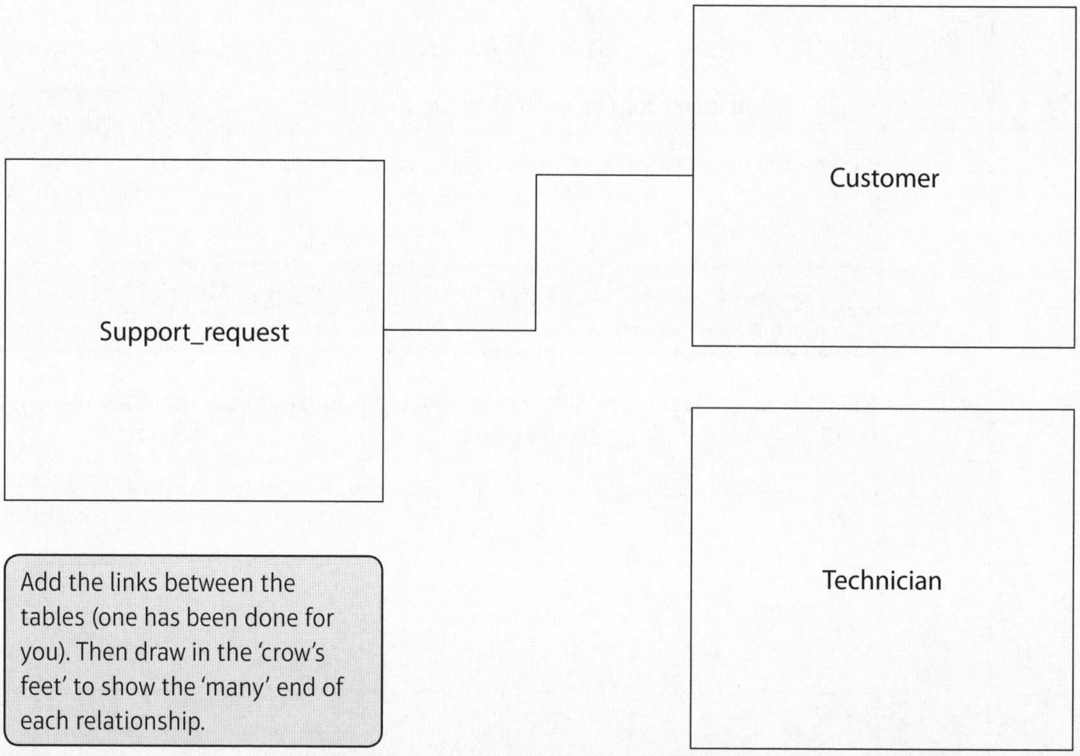

> Add the links between the tables (one has been done for you). Then draw in the 'crow's feet' to show the 'many' end of each relationship.

Links Revise ERDs by looking at page 50 of Unit 2 in the Revision Guide.

Total for Activity 1 = 8 marks

Activity 2: Data dictionary

Produce a data dictionary for your database using the tables below.

You need to complete a **data dictionary** for each table (Support_request, Customer and Technician). The first one or two entries in each table have been made for you.

In your actual set task you will complete this activity on a computer. You will be given an electronic template for the tables and you can duplicate the table, extend the box space and add as many rows as you need.

Table Name:	**Customer**
Field name	**Attributes**
Customer_ID	Primary key, autonumber data type

Remember to:
- make sure the fields are **atomic**. Ask yourself, 'Do any of the fields need to be split into several separate fields?' (look for fields containing data such as names and addresses)
- identify the **primary key** in each table, and the **foreign key** in the tables at the 'many' end of the relationships
- be consistent in your **field naming**
- make sure you include the **data type** and any **validation** necessary in the Attributes column.

Add validation where required. Fields such as a person's name or description of the problem cannot be validated. But use validation for:
- fields with a fixed format – use an input mask
- fields with a limited number of valid entries – use a lookup table
- fields with a datatype of date and/or time – these are automatically validated by Access, but you can use validation to check things such as that the date is not in the future.

Links To revise validation, look at pages 67–69 of Unit 2 in the Revision Guide.

Table Name:	Support_request
Field name	**Attributes**
Request_ID	Primary key, autonumber data type
Customer_ID	Foreign key linking to the customer table. Integer data type

Table Name:	Technician
Field name	**Attributes**
Technician_ID	Primary key, autonumber data type
Technician_f_name	Text data type, 25 characters, no validation

The exact length of text data type fields is not critical as long as they are long enough to contain the intended values.

Links Revise data dictionaries by looking at page 57 of Unit 2 in the Revision Guide.

Total for Activity 2 = 8 marks

Activity 3: Design specification

Complete the 'Design specification document' given below.

Ensure sufficient information is provided for a third party to implement the interface for your solution.

> Make sure you create user interface designs for all the objects (forms, queries and reports) required for the database.
>
> In your actual set task you will complete this activity on a computer. You will be given an electronic template for your designs and you can extend the box space and add as many rows as you need.
>
> Include each design in a separate row.

> All the items you need to produce for the IT support company database are listed below. Some of the designs have been completed for you. Complete the remaining designs.

> Make sure your designs are clear enough for someone else to implement. You need to add annotations so it's clear how the form, report or query will work.

Design specification document:

Name and type	
Type: Form **Name:** Menu This form is not linked to any specific table, it just provides a menu to all the other database facilities. Each button links to the appropriate form, query or report.	**Support request menu** Add support request — **Go** Update support request — **Go** List all unresolved requests — **Go** List a technician's unresolved requests — **Go** Monthly report on requests by technician — **Go** Monthly report on requests by customer — **Go** Report on time taken to resolve requests — **Go**

Type: Form
Name: Add_request

This form allows input of a new support request.
The customer name and technician allocated data is picked up off the Customer and Technician tables, and the primary key field from each of these tables is inserted in the Support_request table as a foreign key.
The Save button saves the record, the Cancel button closes the form without saving the record.

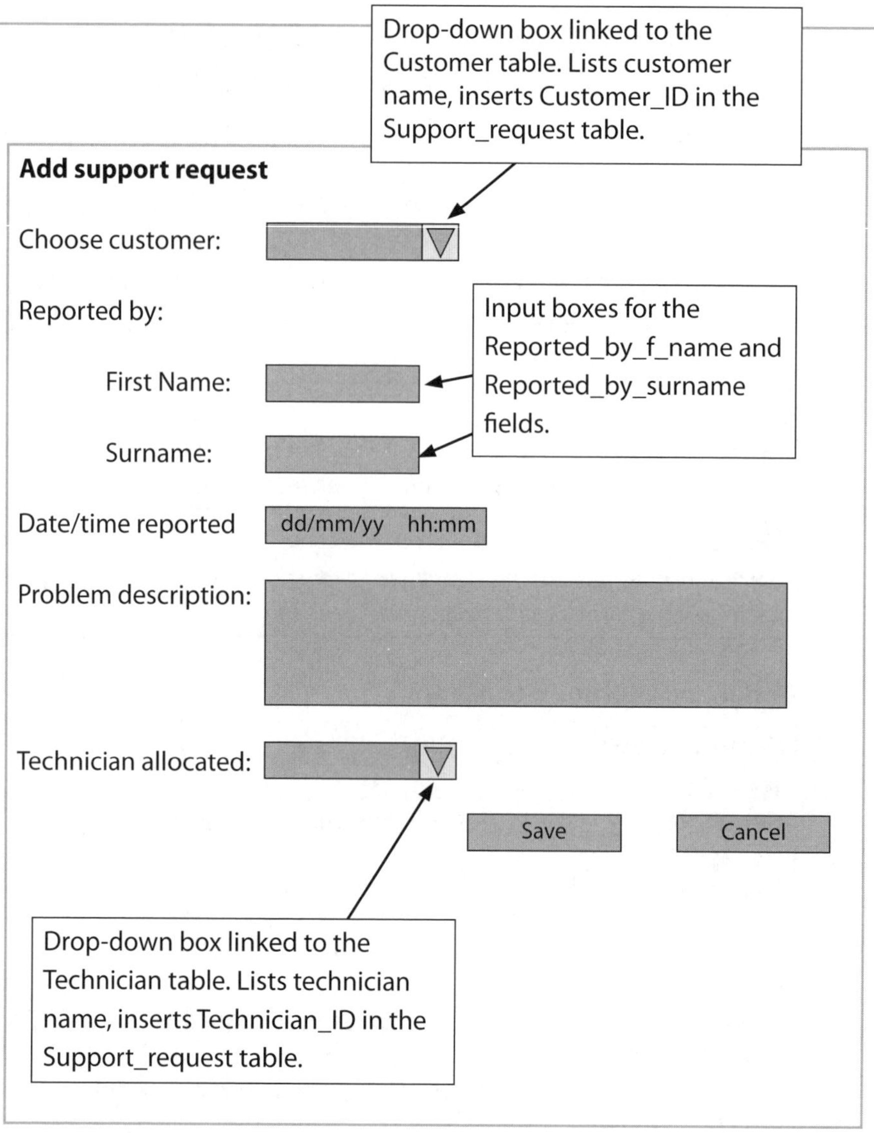

Links Revise form design by looking at page 74 of Unit 2 in the Revision Guide.
Revise adding automated features (such as Save and Cancel command buttons) to forms on page 75 of Unit 2 in the Revision Guide.

This form needs to be based on a query to allow the user to input the request ID of the request they want to update.

Type: Form **Name:** Update_support_request	

The fields shown on the form should be the same as those on the Add_request form, with the addition of fields allowing the user to enter that the request has been resolved, the date and time of resolution and the resolution description.

The user should not be allowed to change all the fields on the form. For example, the customer, the person who reported the query and the date and time reported should be displayed but should be locked so they cannot be changed.

Links

To revise how to use the Locked and Enabled properties on forms see page 74 of Unit 2 in the Revision Guide.

Type: Query
Name: List_all_unresolved_requests

This query lists all unresolved queries. It brings together the Support_request table and the Customer table so the customer name can be listed.

Table	Support_request	Support_request	Customer	Support_request	Support_request
Field	Request_ID	Customer_ID	Customer_name	Problem_description	Resolved
Criteria					No
Sort					

The criterion for this query is on the Resolved field. It is set to 'No' so only requests that have not been resolved are selected.

Make sure you add annotation explaining the criterion or criteria you use for each query.

Type: Query **Name:** List_a_ technician's_ unresolved_requests	

Think about what fields you need to include in your query, and which tables these will come from.

From the Support_request table you will need the Request_ID, the Customer_ID, Problem_description and Resolved fields.

From the Technician table you will need the Technician_surname field.

From the Customer table you should include the Customer_name field.

You will need to include a message box prompting the user to enter the technician's surname.

Remember to set the 'Resolved' field criterion to 'No' so only unresolved queries are listed.

Links Revise query design, including how to add prompt boxes to your criteria, on page 64 of Unit 2 in the Revision Guide.

Type: Report
Name: Monthly report of support requests by technician

This report is based on a query which brings together the Technican, Customer and Support_request tables. The criterion for the query is the month required. The report groups the output by technician, listing each request allocated to that technician in the month in question.

Support requests listed by Technician

Month: June 2016
Technician: Xxxxxxxxxx Xxxxxxxxx

Customer	Date/time reported	Problem	Resolved?
Xxxxxxxxx	dd/mm/yy hh:mm	Xxxxxxxxxxxxxxxxxxxxxxxx	X
Xxxxxxxxx	dd/mm/yy hh:mm	Xxxxxxxxxxxxxxxxxxxxxxxx	X
Xxxxxxxxx	dd/mm/yy hh:mm	Xxxxxxxxxxxxxxxxxxxxxxxx	X

Technician: nnnnnnn nnnnnnn

Customer	Date/time reported	Problem	Resolved?
Xxxxxxxxx	dd/mm/yy hh:mm	Xxxxxxxxxxxxxxxxxxxxxxxx	X

Type: Report
Name: Monthly report of support requests by customer

As well as drawing the design for the report, make sure you include annotation describing the query behind your report.

Which tables will be included in the query and which fields?

What will be the criterion or multiple criteria for the query?
How does the report group the output?

Type: Report **Name**: Report on time taken to resolve requests	

The criterion for the query will be a calculation: Date_time_reported subtracted from Date_time_resolved.
Think too about how you will sort the results.

Links Revise queries using calculated fields by looking at page 64 of Unit 2 in the Revision Guide.
Revise how to design reports by looking at page 63 of Unit 2 in the Revision Guide.

Total for Activity 3 = 6 marks

Activity 4: Testing plan

Use the 'Test log document' given below to plan how you will test your completed database.

The tests for the Customer table have been entered for you.

Create the testing plan using your data dictionary as a guide. Make sure you include tests for every field in the data dictionary. You do not need to add tests for autonumber fields as these are inserted automatically by Access, and you should not change them as they are used for the primary keys.

In your actual set task you will complete this activity on a computer. You will be given an electronic template for the tables and you can extend the box space and add as many rows as you need.

Test log document:

Test number	Purpose of test	Test data	Expected result	Actual result	Comments and action taken
Tests for fields in the Customer table					
1	Customer_name field	Joe Smith and Co	Accepted		
2	Address field	26 The Avenue	Accepted		
3	Town field	Bristol	Accepted		
4	Postcode field	a4bbx	Rejected		
5	Postcode field	BR99 1ZZ	Accepted		

Include tests of the validation in any fields which have validation applied. Remember to include, normal, extreme and erroneous data.

Always include the expected result for each test and check carefully that you've done this correctly.

Links To revise testing plans, look at page 65 of Unit 2 in the Revision Guide.

In the testing plan for the Support_request table, include tests for referential integrity of foreign keys.

Tests for fields in the Support_request table					
6	Customer_ID field referential integrity	9	Rejected (no Customer_ID 9)		
7	Customer_ID field referential integrity	4	Accepted		
	Technician_ID field referential integrity				
	Technician_ID field referential integrity				
Tests for fields in the Technician table					

Links To revise the meaning of referential integrity, look at page 53 of Unit 2 in the Revision Guide. To revise how to enforce referential integrity, look at page 70 of Unit 2 in the Revision Guide.

Total for Activity 4 = 6 marks

Activity 5: Database development and testing

Develop and test your database using the information in the documents you produced for activities 1–4.

Record your database development as annotated screenshots in a single document.

Your screenshots should show:

- your tables, including the fields and attributes
- your table relationships
- your queries, including fields and criteria
- the output of your queries
- the forms you have created
- the reports you have created
- evidence of working validation.

Record your testing including test results, comments and actions taken to resolve issues in the 'Test log document' you created in activity 4.

Database development

You can access the .csv file containing the data for the Harrow FIX-IT database by scanning this link with your smartphone or tablet. Alternatively, go to the following link: http://activetea.ch/2gNTa18. Use this file to create your database. The first task is to import the raw data from the .csv file.

Links Revise how to import data from a .csv file into Access by turning to page 82 of Unit 2 in the Revision Guide.

Guided

1. Look at the screenshots below, provided as evidence for this activity. Complete the student's commentary and annotations by filling in the blanks.

You will need to compile your screenshots and annotations in a separate document.

Look at the next few pages for examples of screenshots you could include, and how you can annotate your screenshots. Read the hints to get more help with creating your database.

You don't have to take a screenshot of every single detail. Just make sure you provide enough annotated screenshots to document the development process.

My database development screenshots.

The first task I completed was to create the (a) ....,

using my data (b) .... as a guide.

Remember to use object names (the names you use for tables and fields as well as forms, queries and reports) which are clear and would enable anyone else looking at the database to see what they are used for.

This is the Customer table.

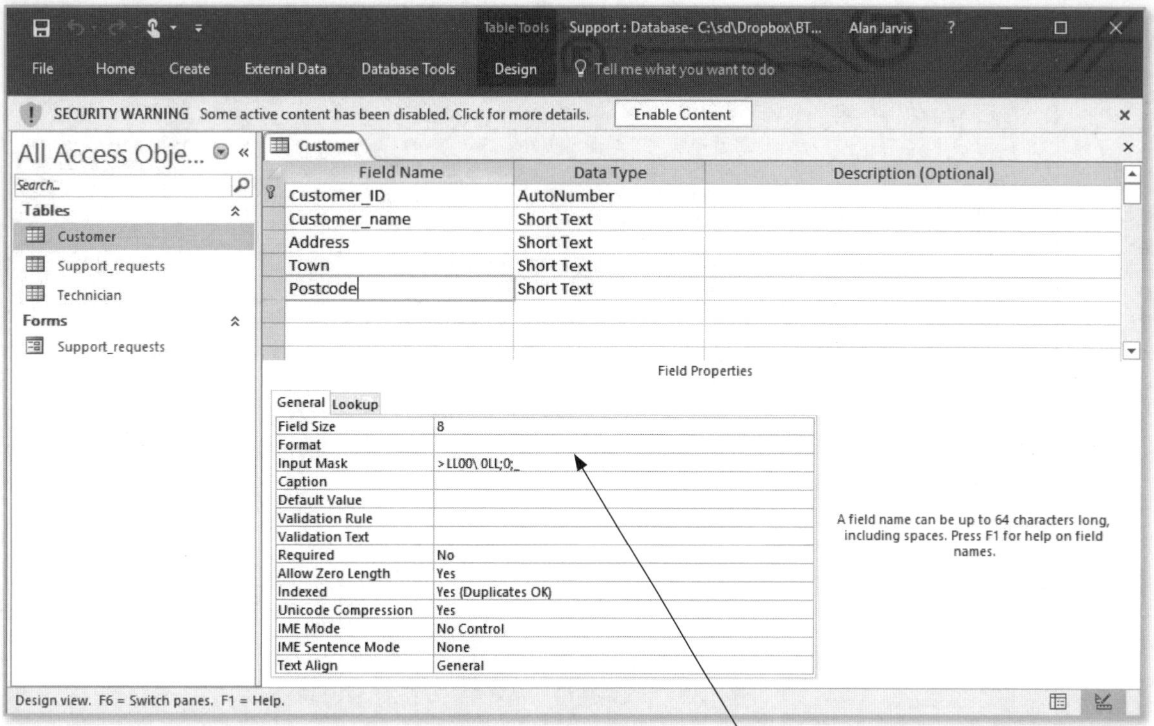

I have added an (c) .... for the Postcode field.

This is the (d) .... table.

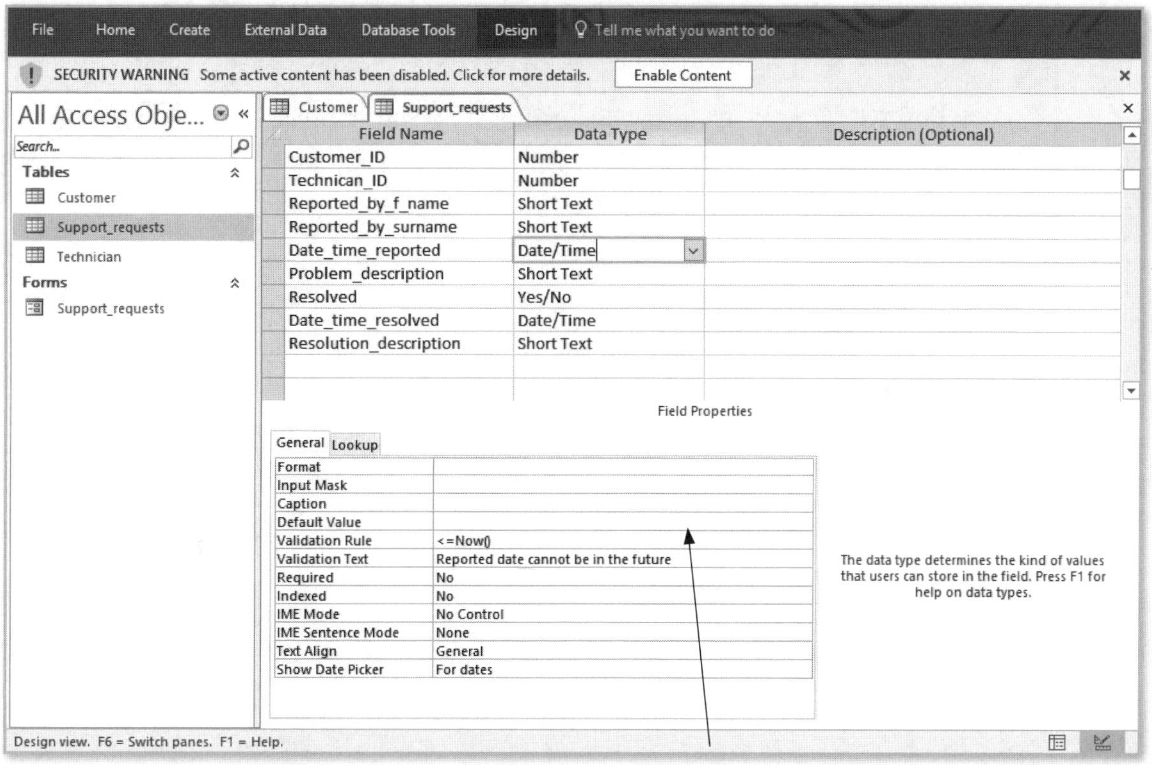

I have added a (e) .... rule with validation text for the Date_time_reported and (f) .... fields.

This is the (g) .... table.

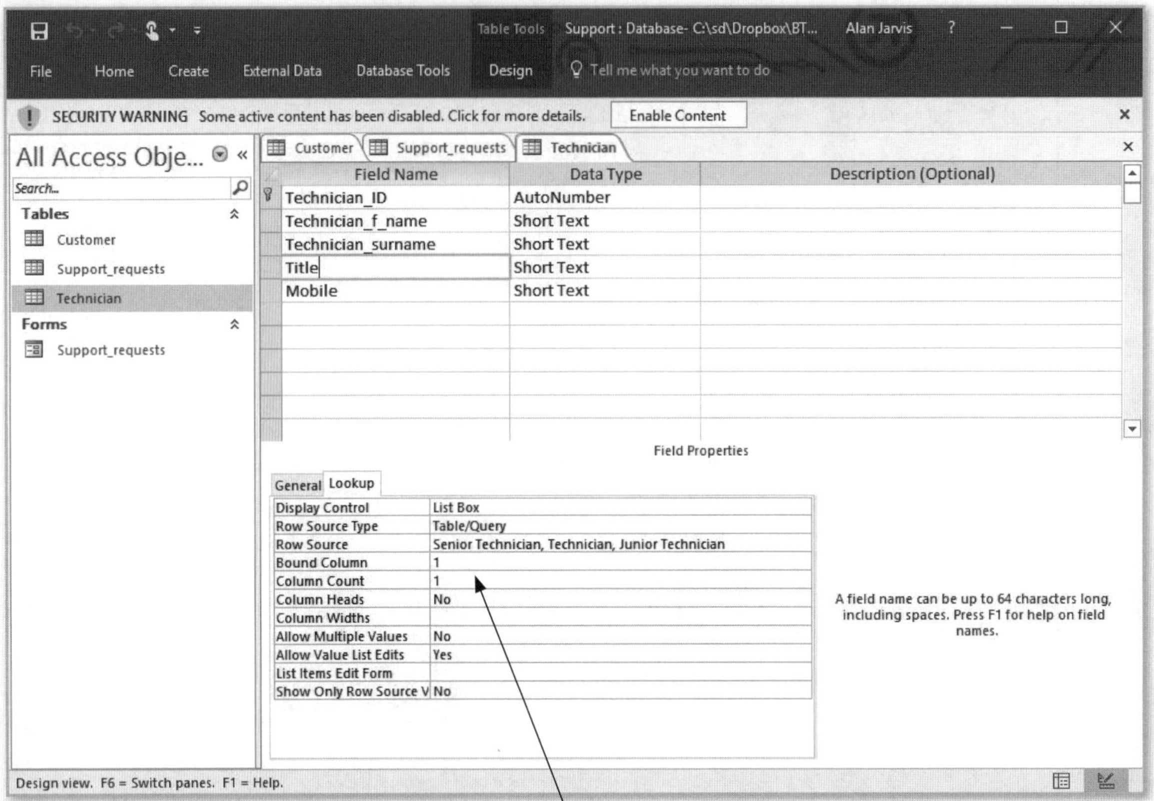

I have used a (h) .... table to provide validation for the

(i) .... field. The list contains three options:

(j) .... Technician, Technician and (k) .... Technician.

2. Next you need to import the data. These are the steps for importing data. Put them into the correct order by writing the numbers 1–4 in the boxes.

☐ Follow the steps in the text import wizard.

☐ From the External Data menu, choose Text file.

☐ Create or open a database.

☐ Find the file you need to import and choose to import it into a new table.

Links To revise importing data, look at page 82 of Unit 2 in the Revision Guide.

3. Look at the student's screenshots of importing the data, and fill in the blanks

Importing data

The next task I completed was importing the sample (a) .... I used the Import Text (b) ....

This is one of the steps in the wizard.

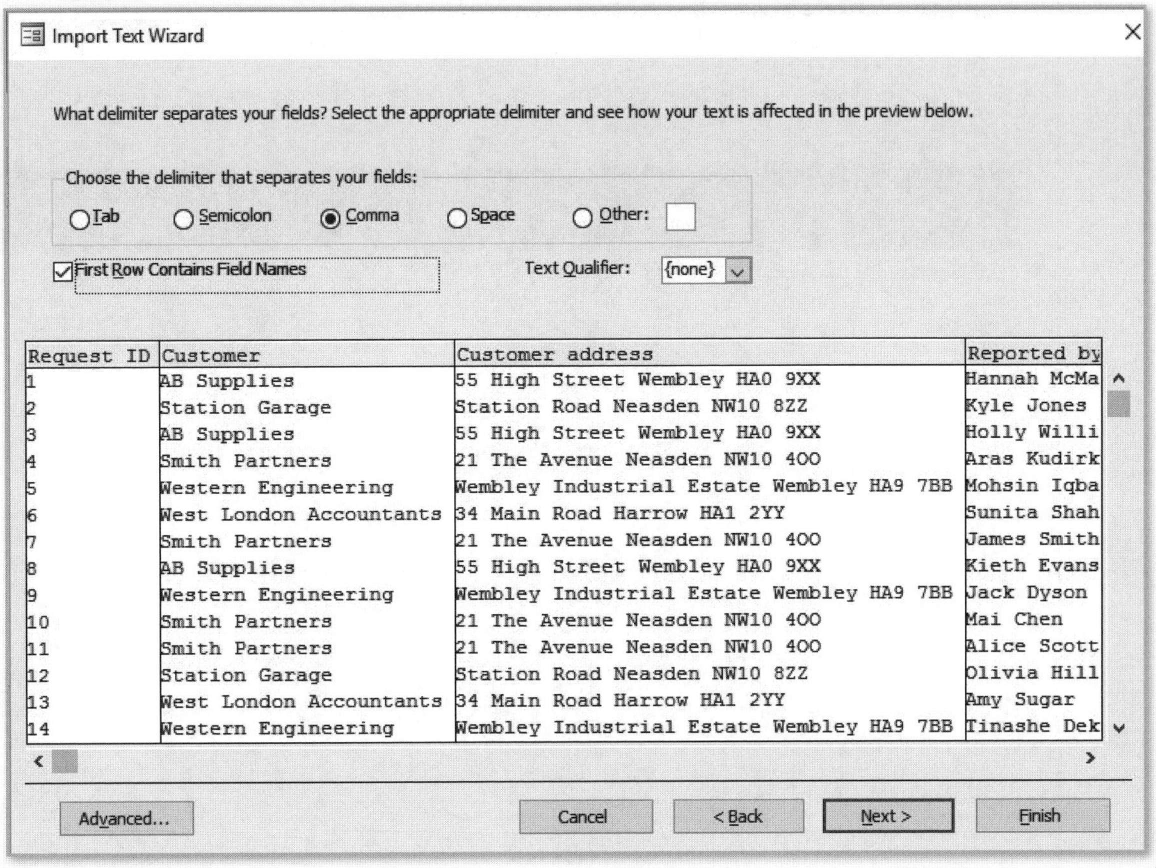

Request ID	Customer	Customer address	Reported by
1	AB Supplies	55 High Street Wembley HA0 9XX	Hannah McMa
2	Station Garage	Station Road Neasden NW10 8ZZ	Kyle Jones
3	AB Supplies	55 High Street Wembley HA0 9XX	Holly Willi
4	Smith Partners	21 The Avenue Neasden NW10 4OO	Aras Kudirk
5	Western Engineering	Wembley Industrial Estate Wembley HA9 7BB	Mohsin Iqba
6	West London Accountants	34 Main Road Harrow HA1 2YY	Sunita Shah
7	Smith Partners	21 The Avenue Neasden NW10 4OO	James Smith
8	AB Supplies	55 High Street Wembley HA0 9XX	Kieth Evans
9	Western Engineering	Wembley Industrial Estate Wembley HA9 7BB	Jack Dyson
10	Smith Partners	21 The Avenue Neasden NW10 4OO	Mai Chen
11	Smith Partners	21 The Avenue Neasden NW10 4OO	Alice Scott
12	Station Garage	Station Road Neasden NW10 8ZZ	Olivia Hill
13	West London Accountants	34 Main Road Harrow HA1 2YY	Amy Sugar
14	Western Engineering	Wembley Industrial Estate Wembley HA9 7BB	Tinashe Dek

Once the data had been imported I used Append queries to split it up into the

(c) .... I created before.

Append queries are similar to standard queries accept that the results of the query are inserted into a new or existing table. You can make any query an append query by selecting the Append icon in the Query Tools Design toolbar.

Here is the Append query I used to put records in the Support_requests table.

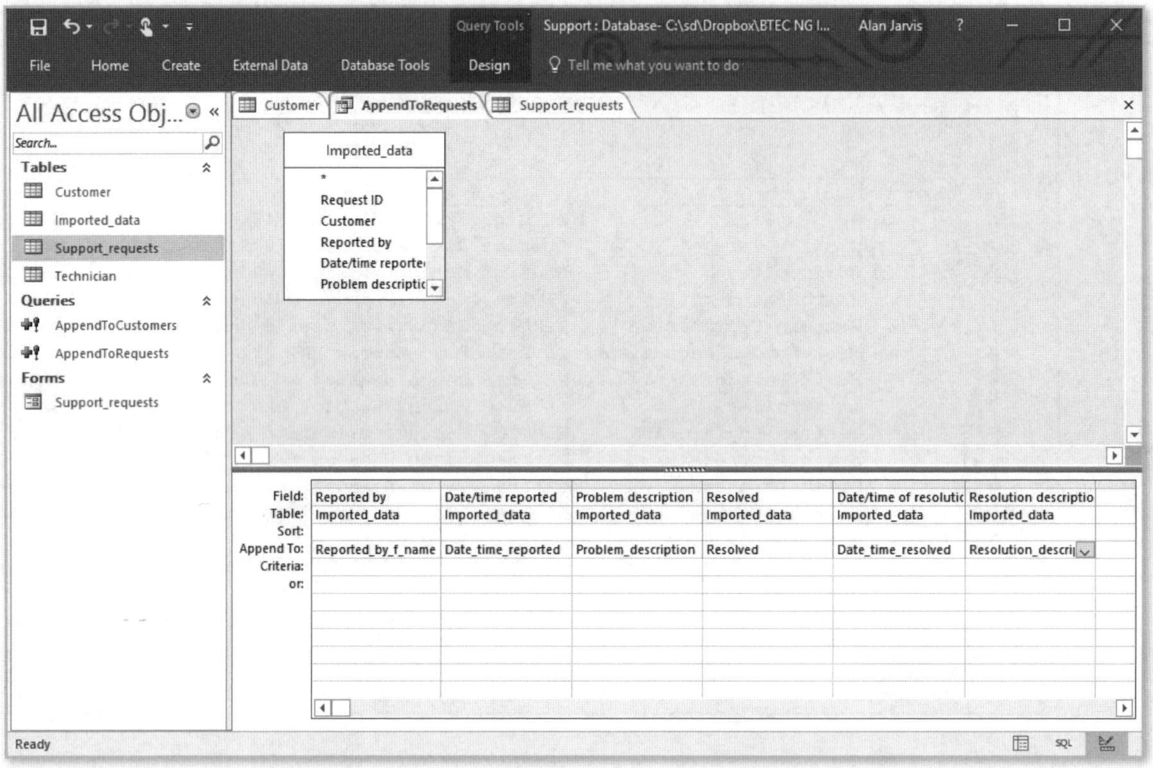

Once the data was imported, I checked the (d) .... keys in the Support_requests table. I was then able to create the (e) .... between the tables. Here are the (f) .... I created.

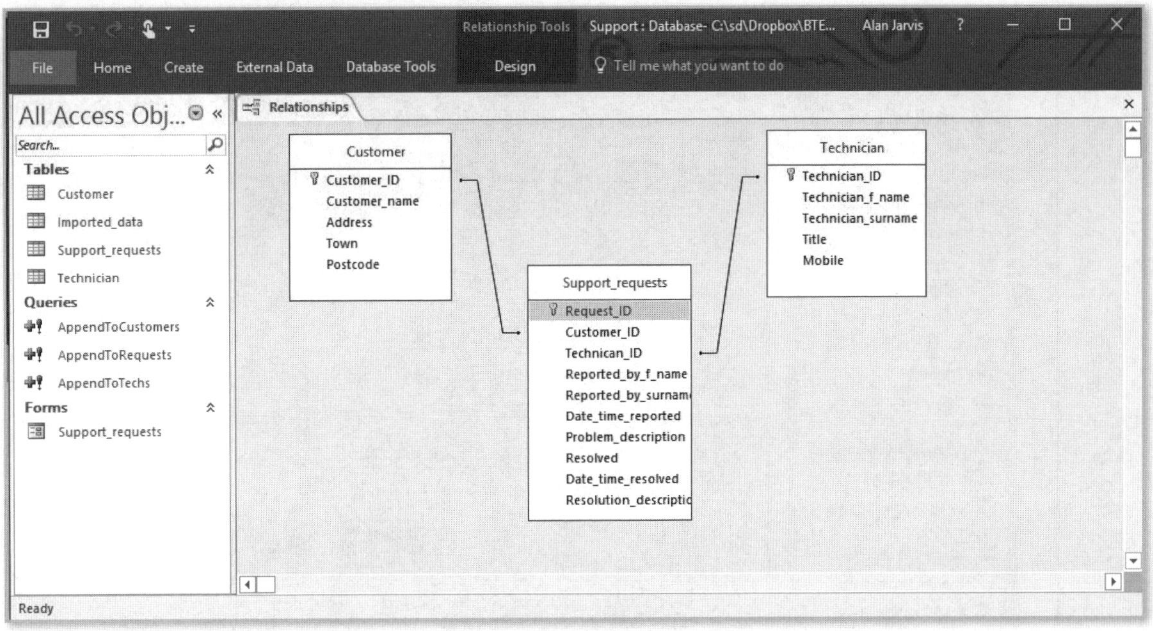

Don't forget to switch on referential integrity when creating the relationships. It's a good idea to include a screenshot of this.

4. Look at the student's screenshots of creating the forms, queries and reports, and fill in the blanks.

Creating the objects

The next task was to create the forms.

This is the Add support request (a) ....

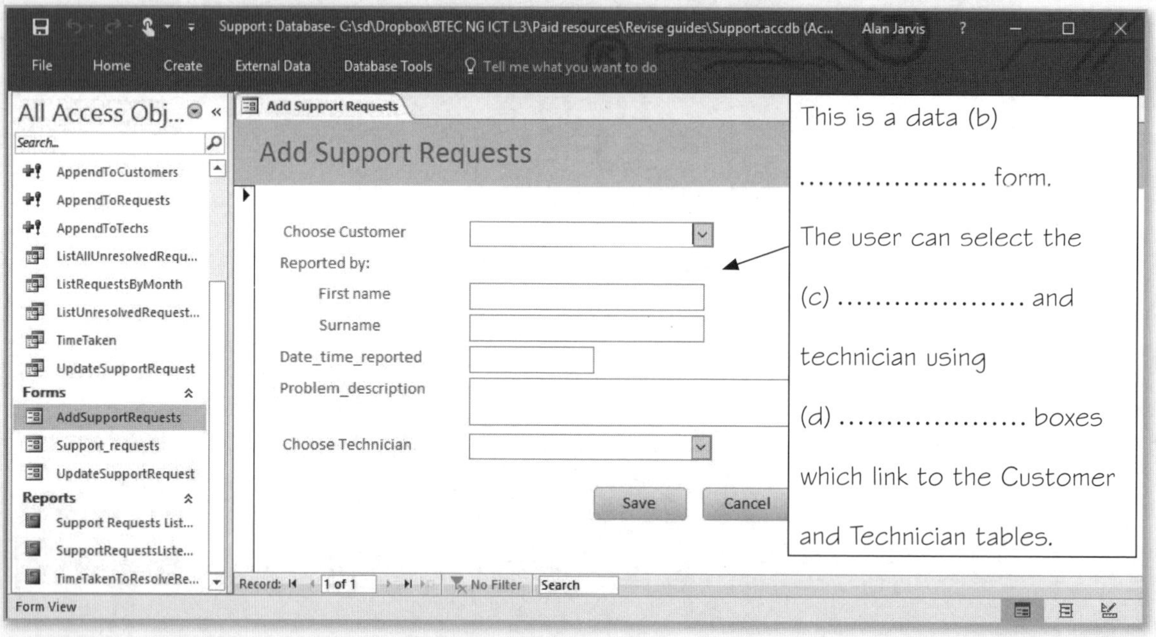

This is a data (b) .... form.

The user can select the (c) .... and technician using (d) .... boxes which link to the Customer and Technician tables.

Your forms need to be intuitive (i.e. it should be obvious how to use them) so make sure everything is clearly labelled and the layout is neat and consistent.

This is the (e) .... form.

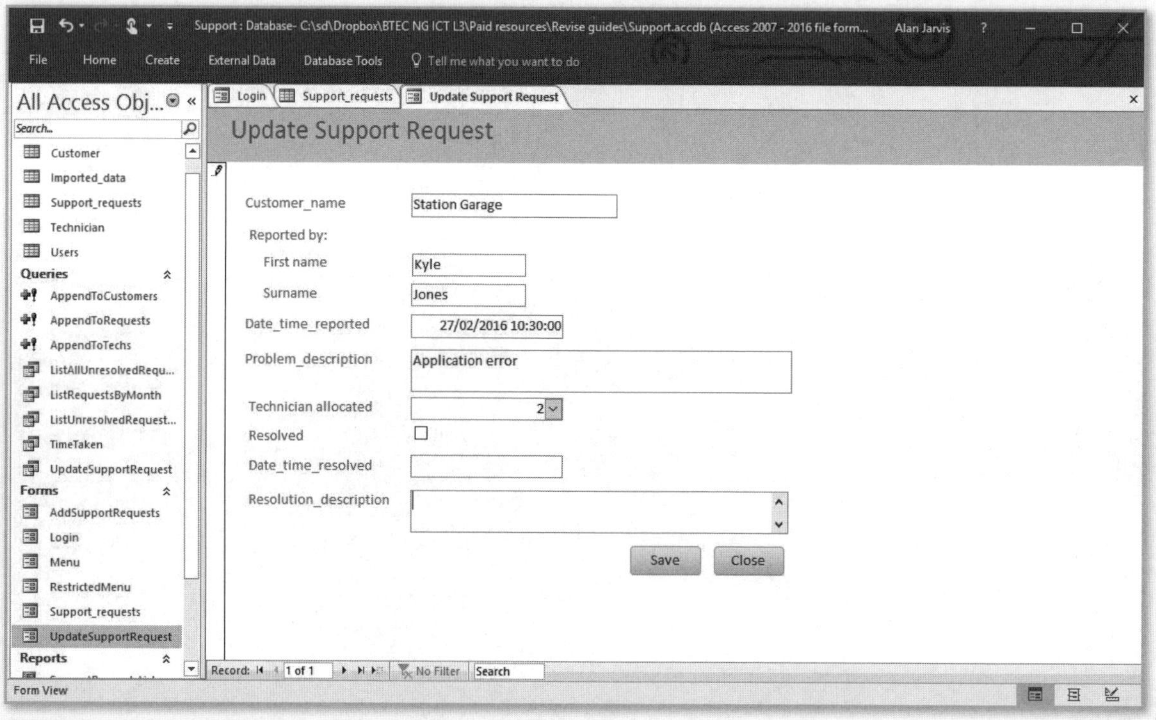

These are the (f) .... I created:

The design view of the (g) .... for listing all unresolved requests looks like this.

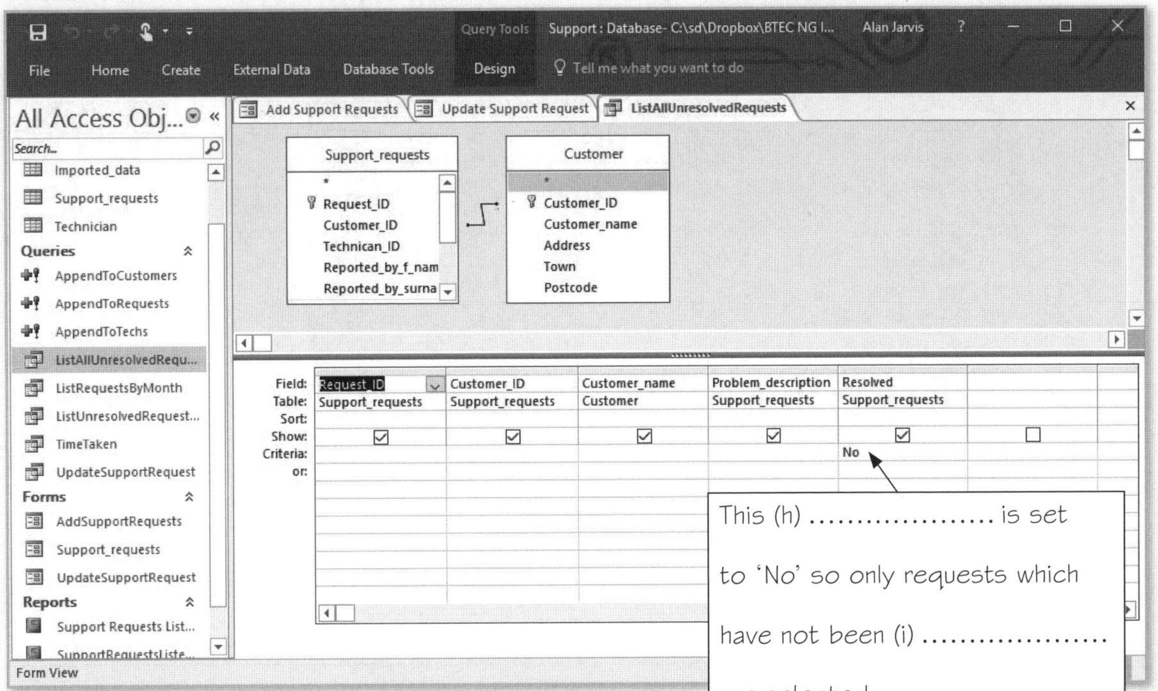

This (h) .... is set to 'No' so only requests which have not been (i) .... are selected.

The (j) .... of the query looks like this.

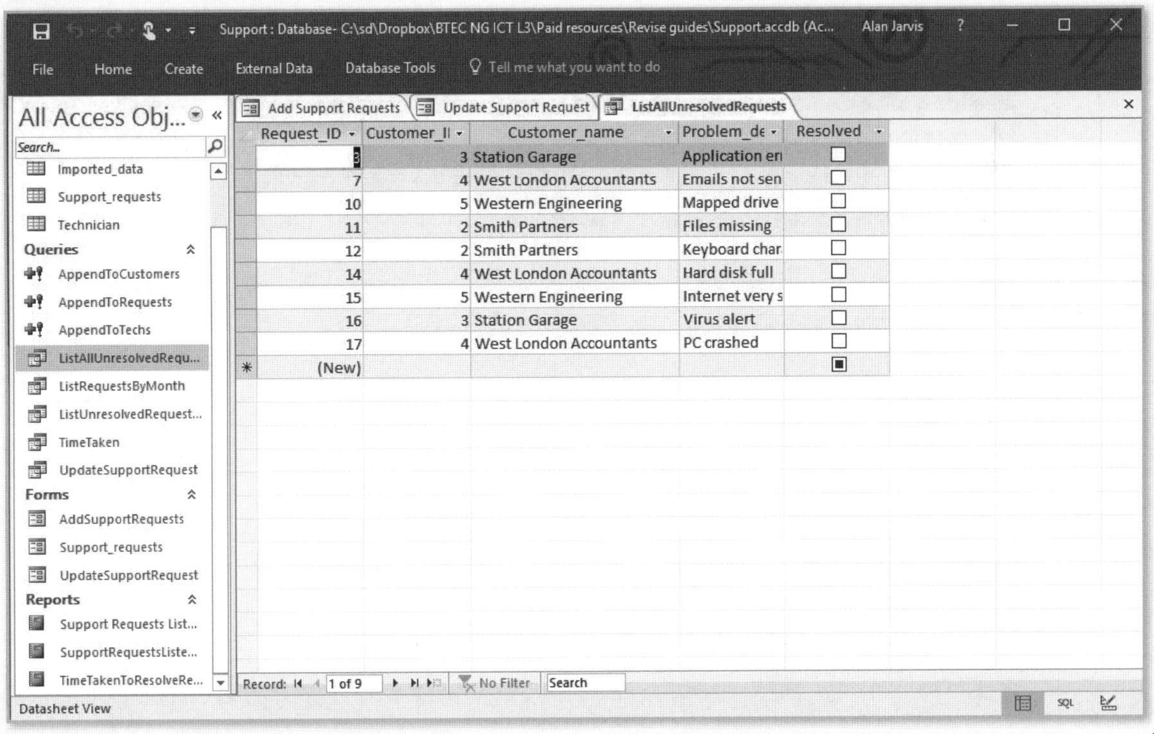

Here is the (k) .... view of the query for listing a technician's unresolved support requests.

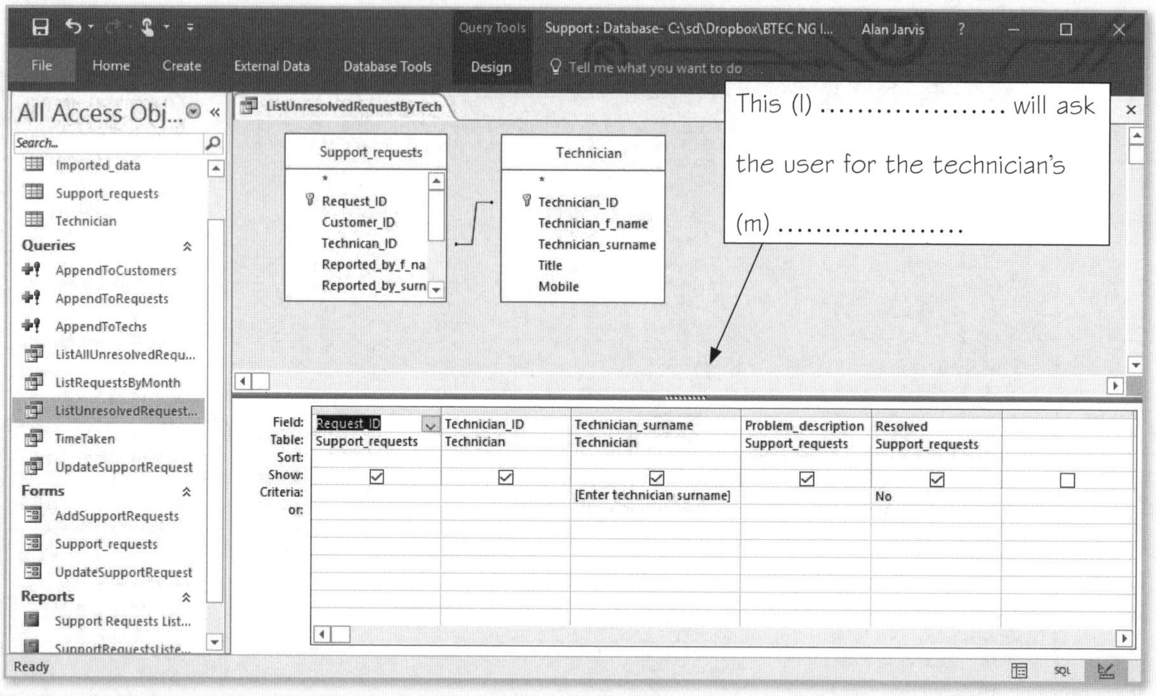

This (l) .... will ask the user for the technician's (m) ....

This is the result when the user enters the surname (n) .... and the query is (o) ....

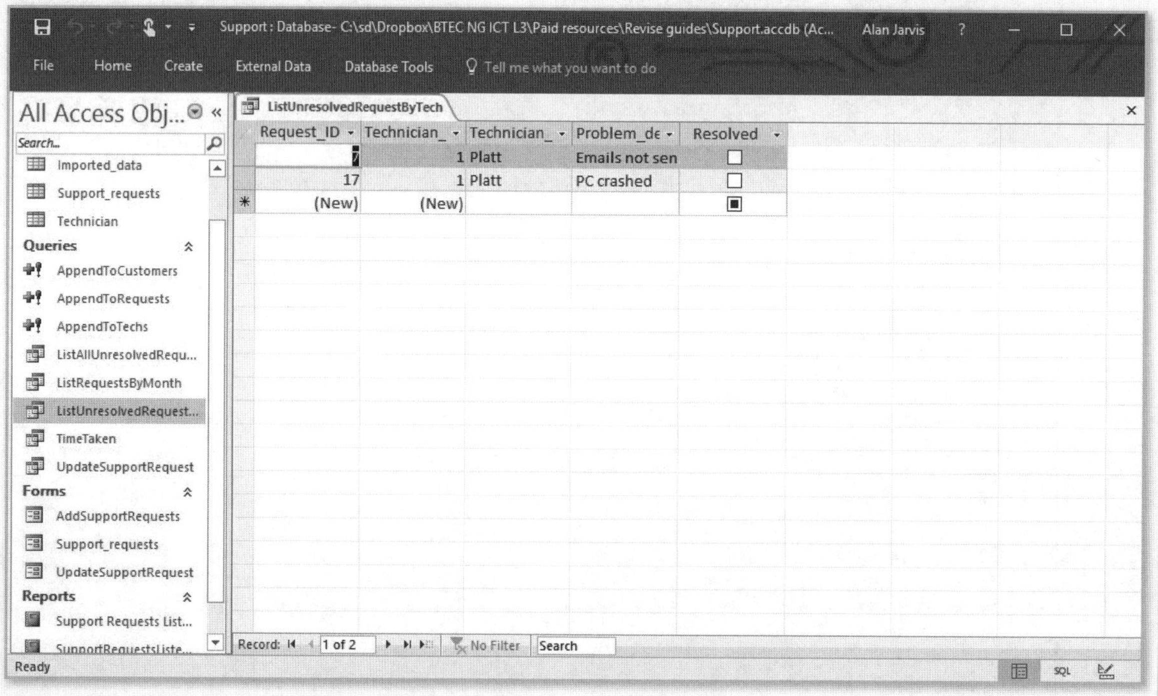

Next I completed my (p) ....

This is the report for listing Support requests by (q) .... To run the report the user enters the number of the (r) .... that they want for the report.

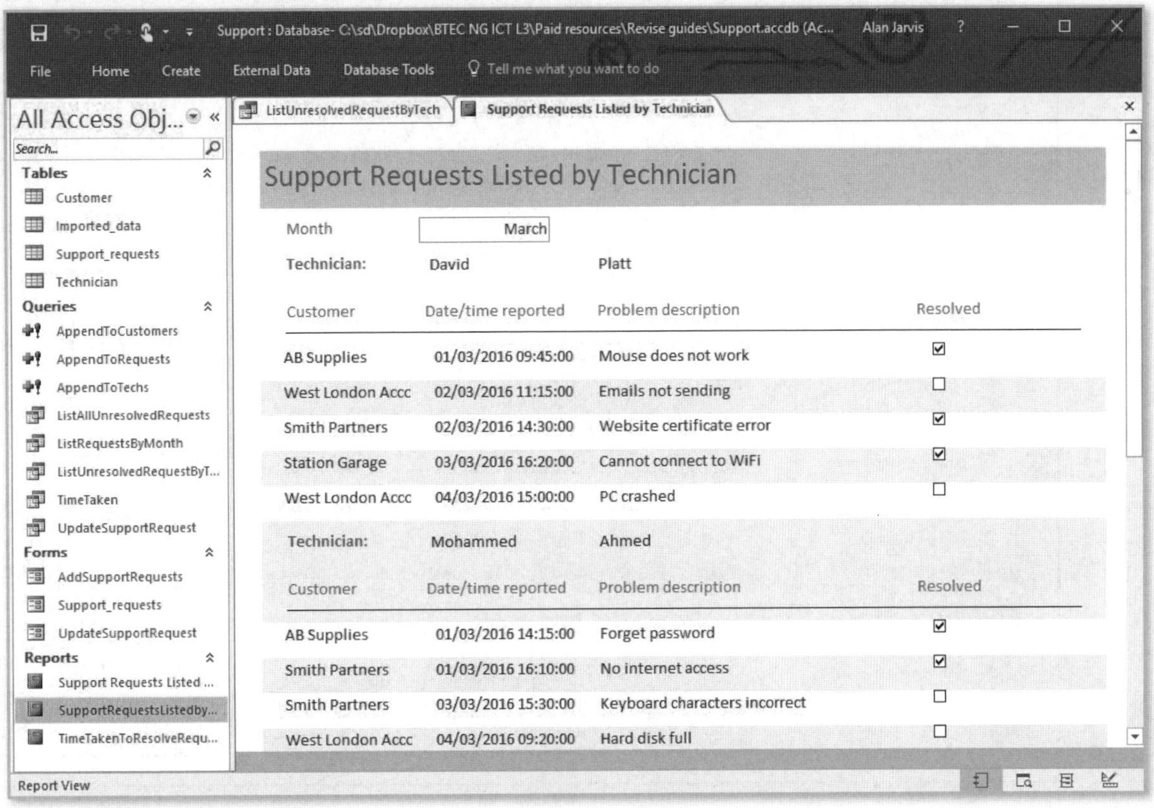

This is the report for listing support requests by (s) ....

The user needs to enter the month number to (t) .... this report.

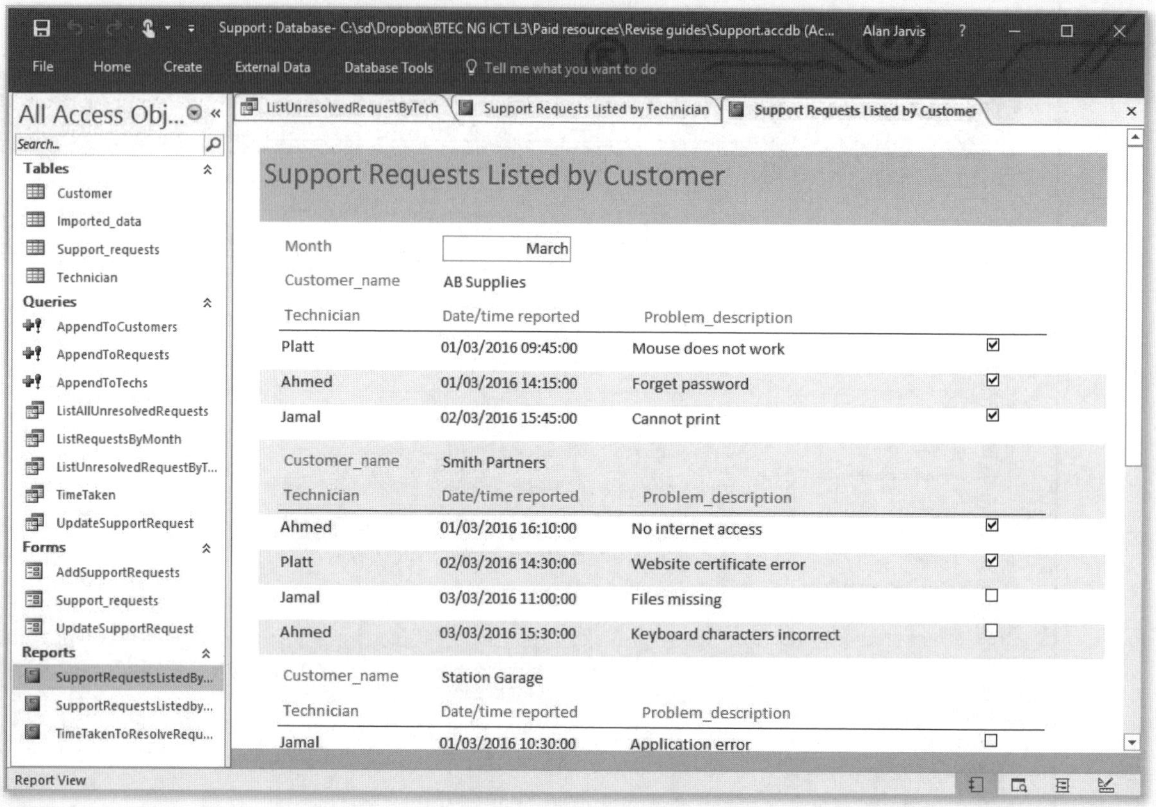

This is the report for showing the (u) .... taken to resolve support requests.

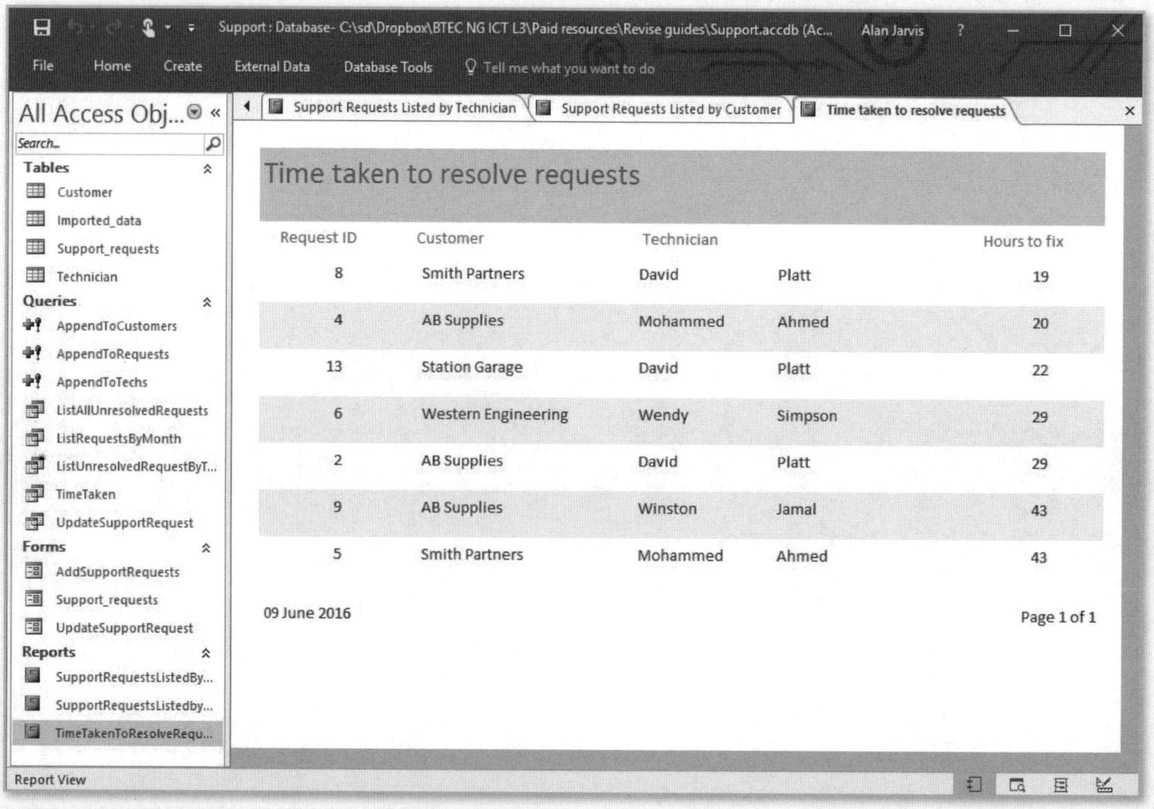

Once all the forms, reports and queries were complete, I created the (v) .... form, which has (w) .... to access all the objects.

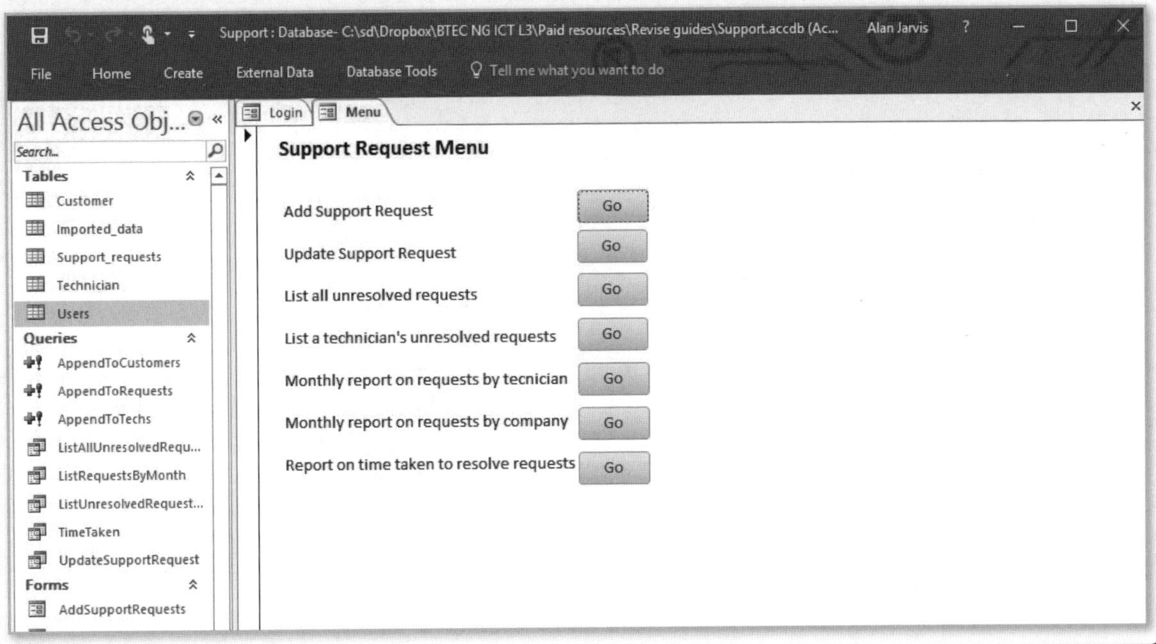

Now create your own database, following the designs you created in activities 1–4. Import the data for your database by scanning this link with your smartphone or tablet. Alternatively, go to the following link: http://activetea.ch/2gNTa18.

Database testing

Record your testing including test results, comments and actions taken to resolve issues in the 'Test log document' you created in activity 4.

As well as the screenshots of your database development you also need to provide screenshots of the testing you carry out on your completed database.

In the actual set task you will need to make a copy of the test plan you created in activity 4 and fill in the 'Actual result' column as you carry out the tests. If you find the actual result does not match the expected result you need to explain that this happened in the comments column, and state what action you took to deal with the problem. This will provide evidence of using an **iterative** development and testing process.

This is an example of the completed test log for the first few tests. The student has added comments explaining the validation and has included a screenshot of the validation.

Test number	Purpose of test	Test data	Expected result	Actual result	Comments and action taken
Tests for fields in the Customer table					
1	Customer field	Joe Smith and Co	Accepted	Accepted	
2	Address field	26 The Avenue	Accepted	Accepted	
3	Town field	Bristol	Accepted	Accepted	
4	Postcode field	a4bbx	Rejected	Rejected	The input mask converts the lower case characters to upper case automatically and will not allow a digit in the second character.
	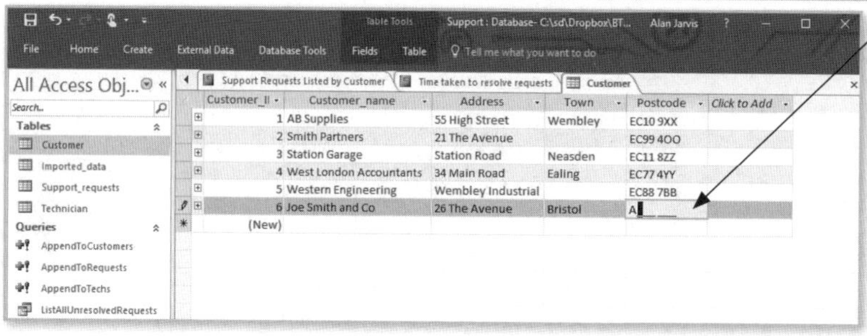				Here you can see the input mask working. Add screenshots showing that any validation you have used works as intended.
5	Postcode field	BR99 1ZZ	Accepted	Accepted	
Your evaluation					

Create a copy of the testing plan you created in activity 4 in a separate document. Carry out your tests on your completed database and record the results, adding comments and screenshots as necessary.

Total for Activity 5 = 26 marks

Activity 6: Evaluation of your database solution

Evaluate your solution.

You should consider:

- how well your solution meets the requirements of the scenario
- the quality, performance and usability of the database
- the changes made during the development and testing process.

Record your response in the evaluation section of the 'Test log document' you created in activity 4.

Guided

1. Read the sample evaluation and insert the heading for each paragraph. Choose the paragraph headings from the box – they are currently in the wrong order.

Write each paragraph heading above the appropriate paragraph.

During testing I discovered that:
Elements of my database that work well are:
Elements of my database I could improve are:
How well my database matches my designs:
I could improve the usability of my database in these ways:
In conclusion,
My database is easy to use because:
My database meets the needs of the brief in the following ways:
My database failed to meet the needs of the brief in the following ways:
Some problems I encountered during development:

Sample evaluation

(a) ....

The database I created has all the features listed in the Task Scenario and all the main features work as they should.

(b) ....

Although all the features work, there are a number of things that would need improving if this database was to be used for real.

(c) ....

There were no errors in the tests I have done. This suggests that I have not tested the database thoroughly enough, and if I had more time I would create a more comprehensive test plan.

(d) ....

Everything is labelled clearly and all the forms have Save and Cancel buttons. The layout for the forms is consistent (same colour scheme and fonts used) and fairly neat. The reports are also neat and consistent and clearly labelled.

(e) ....

Some of the labels on the forms still have the underscores for the field names (e.g. date_time_reported). These should be removed and the name made clear (e.g. Date and time reported).

When the queries are run from the main menu there is no button to return to the menu, so it would be easier to use if the results of the queries where displayed in a form.

On the Update support request form it would be better if, when you click the resolved check box, the date and time resolved field is automatically completed with the current date and time.

When a user wants to update a support request, they need to know the request ID. To improve usability, it would be better if there were other ways to search for a support request, such as by company or person who reported it.

(f) ....

The table structure and relationship links all work fine and the referential integrity options ensure, for example, that a support request record must relate to a record on the customer table. The use of drop-down combo boxes on the form makes the user select a valid customer for each request.

I think the reports also work fine and do not need any improvement.

(g) ....

There is not really enough information on the database about the customer. For example, the name of the person at the company who reported the fault is recorded but not their contact details (email address, phone number, etc).

When reporting a new fault, the date and time reported should have the current date/time inserted automatically.

On the Update support request form the technician allocated is only shown by their ID number. It would be better if their name was shown.

The database should really have another table linked to the Support_request table that allows each update to an individual request to be recorded on a separate record. This would require a complete re-design of how supported requests are updated.

(h) ....

My design mostly matched the database I developed, although I had to change some minor layout features of the forms and reports as I went along. The designs of the ERD and data dictionary were correct and I did not need to modify them.

(i) ....

I had a lot of difficulty getting the query behind the Time taken to resolve requests report to work. At first I just had the date of resolving the request subtracted from the date of reporting it.

This gave me the number of days, when it would make much more sense to give the result as the hours. I spent some time trying to remember how to use a function to display just the hours, and eventually I got it to work.

(j) ....

I think my database does have all the required functions and they work fine. There is a lot more refinement I could do (as described above) if I had more time. I think the database might be OK as a prototype to get user opinions as to what else needs adding, but I don't think it would be very effective for use in real life because of the missing features I have listed. I think the database needs a lot more testing as I didn't really have time to test the forms and queries properly.

Always back up the statements you make with evidence. For example, you will get no marks for saying: 'My forms are easy to use'.
But you will get marks for saying: 'My forms are easy to use because they all have a consistent layout, are clearly labelled so the user knows what to do and what each input box and button is for and they all have OK and Cancel buttons to allow the user to confirm or back out of an action'.

Links To revise evaluating your database design, development and testing, look at pages 78, 79 and 91 of Unit 2 in the Revision Guide.

Write an evaluation of your database in the space below.

In the actual set task, you will enter your evaluation of the whole database design, development and testing process in the box at the bottom of the test log you completed in activity 5.

The guidelines below give one way of structuring your evaluation. You can structure your evaluation as you like, but do make sure it is clear and logical and covers all the points listed in the activity

My database meets the needs of the brief in the following ways:

....

....

....

....

....

....

It failed to meet the needs of the brief in the following ways:

....

....

....

....

....

....

In the first two sections include how well the database you developed meets the requirements of the scenario.

- Does it do all the things that are listed in the Task Scenario, particularly those listed in the bullet points underneath 'You need to:'?
- You may not have managed to get everything working fully. Explain which features you could not get to work and why this happened, for example lack of time or problems you encountered.
- Even if you did manage to get all the features to work, there are almost certainly things that could be improved to make the database better suited to the application.

During testing I discovered that ....

....

....

....

....

....

....

Your testing should help you ensure the quality of the database, but it is unlikely that you will have had time to do very through testing of every aspect of the database, including the forms, queries and reports. It is a good idea to mention this here.

My database is easy to use because ....

....

....

....

....

....

I could improve the usability of my database by ....

....

....

....

....

....

....

You should consider the usability of the system you created.
- Is it intuitive and easy to use?
- What aspects of the menus, forms, queries and reports could be made easier for a novice user to understand and use?
- Are there aspects of the user interface that could be improved? For example, could the forms or reports be laid out better, in a neater and more consistent way?

Elements of my database that worked well are ....

....

....

....

....

....

....

Elements of my database I could improve are ....

....

....

....

....

....

....

Some issues you might cover in these two sections are:
- Did your testing reveal any problems with the database? If so how did you deal with them?
- Imagine a user actually using your database. What might you need to change or add to make it fully functioning?

How well my database matches my design: ....

....

....

....

....

....

....

Did your design prove to be correct or did you need to modify it when you came to develop the database?

Some problems I encountered during development: ....

....

....

....

....

....

....

Were there some parts of the database you could not get working properly?

In conclusion, ...

....

....

....

....

....

....

Total for Question 6 = 12 marks

END OF TASK

TOTAL FOR TASK = 66 MARKS

Revision task 2

Set task brief

Task scenario

Your friend is running a dog show in the local town of Byford and has asked you to create a database to track the dogs being entered to the various competitions in the show.

The competitions are:

- the best behaved dog, which is at 2 pm on the day of the show
- the best groomed dog which is at 3 pm
- the most agile dog which is at 3:30 pm
- the best dog overall which is at 4 pm.

A number of dogs have already been entered. Each owner can only enter one dog, but they can enter the dog into as many competitions as they like.

You need to:

- design a database structure that:
  - includes dog, competition and competition entry data
  - avoids unnecessary duplication of data
  - validates data input to ensure integrity.
- create a robust database with a suitable user interface for your friend to enter new dogs and competition entries and to enter the winning dog for a competition
- import and manipulate the given data
- provide database outputs showing:
  - all dogs entered for a given competition
  - all the competitions that a given dog has been entered for
  - all the dogs of a given breed entered for a given competition
  - all the dogs born after 1/1/2013, sorted by name
  - a report showing the details of the winning dog for a given competition
  - a report showing all the details (including dogs entered) for a given competition sorted by owner name
  - a report for an individual dog showing which competitions a dog has been entered in with the times of these competitions
- test your database, adding data to ensure that the database meets all requirements
- evaluate your database against the given requirements.

This first sub-bullet point gives a strong clue as to the tables you will need in your dog show database

The second bullet point lists the two data entry forms you will need to produce.

You will also need to provide a menu form for accessing all the features of your database.

The sub-bullets under the fourth bullet point list all the queries and reports you will need to produce.

Information

The provided raw data contains the entries that have been made so far for the various competitions in the dog show. Figure 1 shows an extract of the data (you will download the .csv file that includes this data as part of activity 5).

Figure 1

Dog name	Dog breed	Date of birth	Owner first name	Owner surname	Competition category	Time of competition	Competition judge	Competition winner
Shep	German Shepherd	01/10/2010	Kelly	Birch	Best dog	16:00	Alice Wilson	
Shep	German Shepherd	01/10/2010	Kelly	Birch	Best behaved dog	14:00	Simon Jones	
Shep	German Shepherd	01/10/2010	Kelly	Birch	Most agile dog	15:30	Eric Smith	
Lilly	Jack Russell	10/05/2009	Liz	Cartmell	Best groomed dog	15:00	Anita Patel	
Lilly	Jack Russell	10/05/2009	Liz	Cartmell	Best behaved dog	14:00	Simon Jones	
Winston	Pug	20/02/2011	Smita	Shah	Best groomed dog	15:00	Anita Patel	
Winston	Pug	20/02/2011	Smita	Shah	Best behaved dog	14:00	Simon Jones	
Spot	Dalmatian	05/04/2014	Rita	Evans	Most agile dog	15:30	Eric Smith	
Spot	Dalmatian	05/04/2014	Rita	Evans	Best dog	16:00	Alice Wilson	
Holly	German Shepherd	03/09/2012	Sara	Lloyd	Most agile dog	15:30	Eric Smith	
Holly	German Shepherd	03/09/2012	Sara	Lloyd	Best dog	16:00	Alice Wilson	
Holly	German Shepherd	03/09/2012	Sara	Lloyd	Best groomed dog	15:00	Anita Patel	
Buster	Bulldog	16/07/2011	Phil	Myers	Best dog	16:00	Alice Wilson	
Buster	Bulldog	16/07/2011	Phil	Myers	Best behaved dog	14:00	Simon Jones	
Buster	Bulldog	16/07/2011	Phil	Myers	Most agile dog	15:30	Eric Smith	
Honey	Beagle	12/04/2012	Ruth	Hamilton	Best dog	16:00	Alice Wilson	
Honey	Beagle	12/04/2012	Ruth	Hamilton	Most agile dog	15:30	Eric Smith	
Honey	Beagle	12/04/2012	Ruth	Hamilton	Best behaved dog	14:00	Simon Jones	
Milly	Yorkshire Terrier	05/03/2014	Piotr	Janowski	Most agile dog	15.30	Eric Smith	
Milly	Yorkshire Terrier	05/03/2014	Piotr	Janowski	Best groomed dog	15:00	Anita Patel	
Milly	Yorkshire Terrier	05/03/2014	Piotr	Janowski	Best behaved dog	14:00	Simon Jones	
Frisky	Collie	15/02/2011	Nicki	Spencer	Best behaved dog	14:00	Simon Jones	
Frisky	Collie	15/02/2011	Nicki	Spencer	Most agile dog	15:30	Eric Smith	
Scruff	Springer Spaniel	21/03/2013	Rashpal	Kaur	Best dog	16:00	Alice Wilson	
Scruff	Springer Spaniel	21/03/2013	Rashpal	Kaur	Best groomed dog	15.00	Anita Patel	
Sandy	Whippet	23/12/2010	Kieran	Hales	Best behaved dog	14:00	Simon Jones	
Sandy	Whippet	23/12/2010	Kieran	Hales	Most agile dog	15:30	Eric Smith	

Activity 1: Entity relationship diagram

Produce an entity relationship diagram (ERD) for the database by normalising the given data to third normal form.

Draw your ERD in the space below. In your actual set task you will create your ERD in software of your choice and save it as a PDF file.

Look at the first bullet point under 'You need to:' in the set task brief. The first sub-bullet point gives a very strong clue as to the tables needed.

Links Then look at the example data provided in Figure 1 on page 64, and identify the repeating groups.

Always check carefully for the types of relationship that exist between the entities.

Here, there is a many-to-many relationship between the Dog and Competition tables, as one dog can enter many competitions, and one competition can have many dogs entered into it.

Many-to-many relationships are always resolved in the same way. You need to create a link entity (table) between the two tables, which in this case you can call Competition_entries. This table takes the primary key from both the tables it links and uses them as foreign keys. It has a one-to-many relationship with each table (with the 'many' end of the relationship in the link table).

Links To revise how to deal with many-to-many relationships, see page 51 of Unit 2 in the Revision Guide.

Revise the normalisation process by looking at pages 55 and 56 of Unit 2 in the Revision Guide.

Remember to identify the primary key in each table. Which table will require foreign keys, and what should these be?

Links You can revise primary and foreign keys on page 52 of Unit 2 in the Revision Guide.

Total for Activity 1 = 8 marks

Activity 2: Data dictionary

Produce a data dictionary for your database using the tables below.

You need to complete a data dictionary for each table you identified in activity 1. You may not need to use all the rows in each table.

Remember that the 'Attributes' column needs to specify the **data type** of each field and any **validation** you will apply.

Text fields, such as dog's name, cannot be validated but other fields can be. What meaningful validation is it appropriate to apply?

Links You can revise data dictionaries by looking at page 57 of Unit 2 in the Revision Guide.

Table Name:	
Field name	**Attributes**

Links To revise validation, look at pages 67–69 of Unit 2 in the Revision Guide.

Table Name:	
Field name	Attributes

Remember to use consistent **field names** with no spacing between words.

Table Name:	
Field name	Attributes

Total for Activity 2 = 8 marks

Activity 3: Design

Complete the 'Design specification document' given below.

Ensure sufficient information is provided for a third party to implement the interface for your solution.

In your actual set task you will complete this activity on a computer. You will be given an electronic template for your designs and you can extend the box space and add as many rows as you need.

Include each design in a separate row.

Remember to add annotations to your designs, either in the first column of the template or as labels on your sketches.

Read the set task brief on page 63. The hints on that page will help you to identify all the forms, queries and reports you need to design.

Design specification document

Start with your designs for the forms. The set task brief on page 63 specifies three different forms that are needed.

Also remember to include a menu form, so users can access all the facilities from one place

Links Revise form design by looking at page 74 of Unit 2 in the Revision Guide.
Revise adding automated features (such as Save and Cancel command buttons) to forms on page 75 of Unit 2 in the Revision Guide.

Name and type (form, query or report)	Fields used, including relevant details of data entry, calculations, presentation of data and navigation required.
Type:...................................... Name:....................................	

Your annotation should state which table the form/fields link to (where relevant), and describe how the boxes on the form support data validation and help the user to enter the required data.

Name and type (form, query or report)	Fields used, including relevant details of data entry, calculations, presentation of data and navigation required.
Type:...................................... Name:....................................	
Name and type (form, query or report)	**Fields used, including relevant details of data entry, calculations, presentation of data and navigation required.**
Type:...................................... Name:....................................	

Remember to include accessibility features on your forms, where possible.

Name and type (form, query or report)	**Fields used, including relevant details of data entry, calculations, presentation of data and navigation required.**
Type:.................................... Name:....................................	

Now design the queries. The set task brief on page 63 specifies four different queries that are needed.

Choose carefully the fields that you want to be displayed when you run your queries. Only include those that will be useful for the user to see. Make sure you list the correct table for each field.

Links Revise query design, including how to add prompt boxes to your criteria, on page 64 of Unit 2 in the Revision Guide.

The criterion for the first query will need to prompt the user to select the competition they want to view.
Remember to put your prompt in the Criteria row under the required field, and to put it inside square brackets.

Name and type (form, query or report	**Fields and tables used, including relevant details of criteria included, user input of criteria, calculations, presentation of data and sorting required.**
Type:...................................... Name:...................................	

The second query will also need to have a user prompt in the Criteria row. Which field will this link to?

Name and type (form, query or report	**Fields and tables used, including relevant details of criteria included, user input of criteria, calculations, presentation of data and sorting required.**
Type:..................................... Name:....................................	

The third query requires two user prompts as criteria, to select the dog breed and competition.

Name and type (form, query or report	Fields and tables used, including relevant details of criteria included, user input of criteria, calculations, presentation of data and sorting required.
Type:..................................... Name:....................................	

For the final query you will need to use a comparison symbol in your criterion for the Date_of_birth field. Don't forget the sort.

Name and type (form, query or report	Fields and tables used, including relevant details of criteria included, user input of criteria, calculations, presentation of data and sorting required.
Type: .... Name:	

Now design your reports. The set task brief on page 63 specifies three different reports that are needed.

Links Revise how to design reports by looking at page 63 of Unit 2 in the Revision Guide.

The first report needs to select the winning dog for a given competition. First create a query which will ask the user to enter the competition (you do not need to show the design for the query, but you can if you wish). Then create a report to format and display the results of the query,

You can design this report as a certificate to give to the winning dog's owner.

Name and type (form, query or report)	Fields used, including relevant details of data entry, calculations, presentation of data and navigation required.
Type:.................................... Name:...................................	

The second report will be a list for the judges so they know which dogs are in the competition they are judging.

Name and type (form, query or report)	Fields used, including relevant details of data entry, calculations, presentation of data and navigation required.
Type:.................................... Name:...................................	

Design the final report as an information sheet for owners.

Name and type (form, query or report)	Fields used, including relevant details of data entry, calculations, presentation of data and navigation required.
Type:.................................... Name:..................................	

Total for Activity 3 = 6 marks

Activity 4: Testing plan

Use the 'Test Log document' given below to plan how you will test your completed database.

In your actual set task you will complete this activity on a computer. You will be given an electronic template for the tables and you can extend the box space and add as many rows as you need.

You need to include a range of data to test any validation for the fields listed in your data dictionary. Where fields have no validation, you can test that data can actually be input to the field – you do not need to include a range of different test data for these fields.

Test log document

Test number	Purpose of test	Test data	Expected result	Actual result	Comments and action taken
Tests for fields in the .... table					
Tests for fields in the .... table					
Tests for fields in the .... table					

Links To revise testing plans, look at page 65 of Unit 2 in the Revision Guide.

Total for Activity 4 = 6 marks

Activity 5: Database development and testing

Develop and test your database using the information in the documents you produced for activities 1–4. Record your database development as annotated screenshots in a single document.

Your screenshots should show:

- your tables, including the fields and attributes
- your table relationships
- your queries, including fields and criteria
- the output of your queries
- the forms you have created
- the reports you have created
- evidence of working validation.

Work through the bullet points one by one as you create your database to make sure you include all the screenshots needed.

Annotate the screen shots clearly to explain what they show. The document you produce for this activity should provide a clear 'story' of your database development.

You will need to use database software to create your database. The first task is to import the raw data from the .csv file.

Links To revise developing your database, refer to pages 66–76 of Unit 2 in the Revision Guide.

You can download the .csv file containing the data for the dog show database by scanning this link with your smartphone or tablet. Alternatively, go to the following link: http://activetea.ch/2fSK0vG.

Links To revise importing data, look at page 82 of Unit 2 in the Revision Guide.

Record your testing, including test results, comments and actions taken to resolve issues in the 'Test log document' you created in activity 4.

Fill in the 'Actual result' column as you carry out the tests. Add comments in the final column where necessary, recording the action you take to resolve unexpected results.

Remember to take notes throughout the development and testing stage to use when you write your evaluation.

Links To revise testing your database, refer to page 77 of Unit 2 in the Revision Guide.

Total for Activity 5 = 26 marks

Activity 6: Evaluation of your database solution

Evaluate your solution.

You should consider:

- how well your solution meets the requirements of the scenario
- the quality, performance and usability of the database
- the changes made during the development and testing process.

Record your response in the evaluation box below.

In the actual set task you will enter your evaluation in the 'Your evaluation' box on the 'Test log document' that you created in activity 4.

Remember to use the 'point and explain' method in your evaluation: make a point, then explain it.

Your evaluation

You could use the bullet points from the activity 6 instructions as headings to help you structure your evaluation. For example:

- How well does my solution meet the requirements of the scenario?
- Evaluation of the quality, performance and usability of the database
- Evaluation of the changes made during the development and testing process
- Conclusion

Alternatively, you could use the paragraph beginnings used in the sample evaluation for Practice task 1 (see page 57) or choose your own way of setting out the evaluation – as long as it covers all the points required.

Links To revise evaluating your database design, development and testing, look at Revision Guide, Unit 2, pages 78 and 79, and page 90.

Total for Activity 6 = 12 marks

END OF TASK

TOTAL FOR TASK = 66 MARKS

Answers

Unit 1: Revision test 1

(Other answers will be possible if they cover similar points. The suggestions that follow are not prescriptive. Answers may cover some/all of the indicative content but you can reward other relevant answers.)

1 (a) (1 mark for each identification and 1 additional mark for each appropriate expansion, up to a maximum of 2 marks each.)

- Mobile devices such as smartphones and tablets use mobile internet connections (1), which allow the technicians to look up problems, combine with GPS and software to use online maps to navigate to jobs, or update the job card while out of the office. (1)
- Mobile devices are also extremely portable (1), which makes it easier for the technicians to carry and use these devices while travelling to repair jobs. (1) **(4)**

(b) (Marks are allocated based on the depth and quality of answers. To ensure maximum marks, you should make appropriate use of technical language and have reasoning that is technically accurate.)

- Laptops are portable computing devices (1) which are able to run diagnostic software (1) and potentially connect to problematic hardware more easily than a mobile device (1).
- A laptop has a separate keyboard, as well as a large screen and a touchpad. (1) These will make it easier to input and gain output from the device (1), so the technicians can provide more detailed updates and feedback on problems. (1) **(6)**

(c) Provide an evaluation of the impact on Excelsior IT Support of the legal, moral and ethical issues, stating if you think the impacts will be largely positive or negative. Your evaluation should be supported by relevant points which may include:

Legislation

- The Data Protection Act requires that organisations keep personal data secure. If the business was found to be in breach of the Data Protection Act by the Information Commissioner then they could be subject to a large fine, potentially hundreds of thousands of pounds.
- In order to comply with the Data Protection Act, the business will need to implement the necessary security measures, including technology, training and procedures, which could be very costly.
- However, the Data Protection Act can make consumers more confident about supplying their data to a business, which makes it easier for the business to perform their activities.
- The Computer Misuse Act provides a mechanism to prosecute offenders that attempt to gain unauthorised access to a computer system and who wish to steal or damage the data stored on those systems.
- Such offences can be punished with up to ten years in jail and a large fine.
- This act benefits the business by deterring individuals from attempting to harm the business's systems.

Moral and ethical issues

- Privacy of individuals should be maintained. An individual's data could be misused for many reasons (e.g. identity fraud) which would seriously negatively affect their life.
- The business has a moral (as well as legal) duty to define and enforce the acceptable use of the data stored on their computer systems to avoid misuse by an employee, such as being shared with someone who should not have access. The business is morally (as well as legally) obliged to protect data being transmitted over the internet, by taking measures such as using appropriate encryption.
- The use of portable storage devices can lead to negative environmental impacts in the form of techno trash due to the regular replacing of hard drives, as these devices are prone to damage. **(12)**

2 (a) (1 mark for each identification and 1 additional mark for each appropriate expansion, up to a maximum of 2 marks each.)

- **Social media** websites allow businesses to create and share information and to **network**. One example is the use of business pages (1) which would allow A2B Taxis to **advertise** deals directly to customers. (1)
- **Blogs** are regularly updated websites that are often used by businesses to share **up-to-date** news and information. (1) A2B Taxis could use this method to inform customers of improvements and innovations in the **services** they offer. (1)
- **Forums** are online discussion sites (1) which could be used by the taxi business to gain customer **feedback** on their goods or services. (1) **(6)**

(b) Provide an analysis of the potential impact of online communities on A2B Taxis, supported by relevant points which may include the following.

Positive impacts

- Better communication with customers – online communities allow direct communication between a business and its customers, such as to gain feedback on services.
- Advertising – online communities provide excellent marketing opportunities, allowing businesses to target customers based on their specific interests.
- Understanding customer needs – strong communication links allow businesses to find out about customer needs more effectively and release new services/products to meet those needs.

Negative impacts

- Cost – setting up online communities, such as a blog or forum, requires an investment in order to develop the systems and maintain them correctly, for example, hiring staff to run the online community.
- Timescales – setting up a new online community takes a long time in terms of development and implementation, and it may take some time before users start taking part in the community.
- Security – online communities can be infiltrated by hackers who try to gain access to the personal data kept on users, so protection is needed against this. **(10)**

(c) In-car navigation systems have become a major part of the service provided by taxi companies like A2B Taxis because they can be used by taxi drivers to ensure they find the destinations, take the quickest route and avoid roadworks and traffic jams, thus providing a better service.

- Mobile devices, specifically smartphones, would be useful to A2B taxis as they can be used by drivers to keep in touch with head office regarding new pickups required or emergencies. The built-in GPS can be used for satellite navigation.
- Personal computers could be used in the offices of A2B Taxis to help them keep track of fares, maintain company finances, contact suppliers, etc.
- Communication devices used for internet access would also be of benefit for allowing the use of email and web

services in the head office. Can maintain a website to advertise the business online.

Additional guidance

- Any reasonable response that relates to the use of digital devices to the efficient running of a taxi business is also acceptable.
- Generic answers about business uses of digital devices are not acceptable. **(10)**

3 (a) You should consider how using cloud storage services will be beneficial when sharing documents.

- Cloud storage services would allow the finance company to share access to folders... and facilitate collaborative working, allowing employees in different locations to work simultaneously on the same project. Employees could be more effective by not having to wait until they return to the office to update or access important documents.
- Employees could access the files while away from the office computers... allowing them to continue to work remotely without the same security implications of using email attachments or portable media, such as USB sticks.
- Cloud storage would make it easier for employees to work on the same documents... eliminating potential issues presented by different users working on their own copies and then trying to combine them at a later date. Users could simultaneously access the same document.

(b) (1 mark for each identification and 1 additional mark for each appropriate expansion, up to a maximum of 2 marks each.)

- A local area network can be used to share a printer (1) so several employees can all make use of the same device. (1)
- A local area network could provide security (1) by having a server and logins rather than standalone machines. (1) **(4)**

(c) Provide an analysis of whether Benjamin's business would benefit from using cloud computing software, supported by relevant points which may include the following.

Advantages

- Software management – the software is not installed on the business's computers so less time and money is needed for managing the software, such as running updates, therefore all employees would be working with the latest/same version of software to prevent any potential conflicts.
- Hardware requirements – cloud computing software runs on the service provider's servers and not the individual workstations, so a business can use cheaper, less powerful computers.
- Flexibility – businesses can adapt to their needs, whether in growth or shrinking in size, by easily increasing or reducing access to cloud computing services.

Disadvantages

- Access to software – if the business's internet connection is down then the software will not be accessible to be used, which leads to loss of productivity.
- Security – the business has no control over the updating of software and security practices for the data stored, which could lead to security issues.
- Ongoing costs – cloud computing software is usually a subscription service, which means increased ongoing costs for running the business.
- Features – *sometimes* cloud based software has reduced feature sets, when compared with their desktop equivalents. **(10)**

4 (a) (1 mark for each identification and 1 additional mark for each appropriate expansion, up to a maximum of 2 marks each.)

- Bandwidth is the rate of data transfer over a network. (1) High bandwidth is required to transfer the large amounts of data in a high-definition video file. (1)
- Latency is the time delay for a data packet to transfer to its destination. (1) Low latency is required to avoid buffering (ensure that video reaches your computer as fast as it is playing). (1) **(4)**

(b) The response may look like the following, but other answers are also acceptable if they cover similar points.

You should consider how using different file types will affect the suitability for streaming video content.

- One file format that is commonly used for videos is the .avi format. This would potentially be of use to Jessica as it would provide very high-quality video. The drawback for Jessica of this file type is that it has a large file size that would take a long time to download.
- Another file format for videos is the .mp4 format. This would be of use to Jessica as it is very good for streaming video over the internet. The drawback for Jessica of using this file type is that its file sizes are still quite large when compared to many other compressed file formats.

Other acceptable formats are:

- MOV is a compressed or uncompressed format designed for use with Apple QuickTime.
- MKV supports high-quality video playback, but is not well supported by some devices, e.g. iPads cannot play .mkv files (any other suitable formats could be included, such as FLV; this list is not exhaustive). **(6)**

(c) Compression is used to reduce the amount of data required to store a file. By compressing the video files Jessica will use less bandwidth when uploading the videos and users will not have to worry about downloading large video files. Her videos should still have the same impact and detail but ultimately take up less space and place less demand on network connections. It may place some load on Jessica's machine as she compresses the files though.
There are two types of compression that are used. One is lossy, the other is lossless. Lossy compression is where the file size is reduced but also some actual video content is lost in the process. It may not be immediately visible but sometimes colours can appear blocky or some fine detail may be lost. Even when uncompressed the original video file cannot be retrieved.
An extremely important tool for compressing video files for transmitting over a network is a codec.
This is used to decipher the compressed video on a user's machine so they can watch the video. Codecs are available for a wide range of compression formats and machines, some may be more efficient than others though and some may allow streaming (watching the video before it has all downloaded) and some may not. **(12)** (Marks are awarded based on the content and quality of the whole answer. You can maximise your potential for achieving all available marks by fully answering the question posed, using appropriate technical language and considering viewpoints with confidence and detail.)

Unit 1: Revision test 2

1 (a) (1 mark for each identification and 1 additional mark for each appropriate expansion, up to a maximum of 2 marks each.)

- PNG files can store transparent colours (1), allowing Lloyd to create 2D graphics that are partially visible or completely transparent so they match the rest of the interface. (1)

- PNG files use lossless compression (1), so if Lloyd wants to increase the quality of the image back to an uncompressed form, he can do so. (1) **(4)**

(b) Analyse the features of the two computers to assess their suitability for use in creating and editing computer graphics.

Processor

- Computer 1 has a quad-core processor which means it can simultaneously perform more operations albeit at a slower speed than the dual-core processor in computer 2, despite computer 2's faster clock speed.
- Graphics editing tasks are often very processor intensive and so the more powerful quad-core processor would help with these tasks.

RAM

- Computer 1 has twice the amount of RAM as computer 2, which means it can store more instructions ready for processing and more data while it is being worked on.
- Graphics editing tasks often require a lot of RAM, as the software requires a lot of RAM to run and graphics files that are in use take up a lot of RAM.

Storage

- Computer 1 has 1 TB of storage compared to 250 GB in computer 2. Graphics files require a large hard disk for storage as files are often very large.
- Computer 2 uses a solid state drive which will make loading and saving the files quicker than computer 1's hard disk drive.

Graphics

- Computer 1 has a 4 GB dedicated graphics card, which is important for graphics editing tasks, particularly 3D modelling, which is very graphics-processing intensive.
- Computer 2 has an integrated graphics card, which uses main memory for storing instructions for graphics processing. The main memory will struggle with the kinds of tasks that Lloyd needs to complete. **(8)**

(c) Features

- Accessibility – files are available to be accessed on any internet connected device with appropriate capabilities, from digital photo frames for display to desktop devices for editing.
- Scalability – easy to increase or decrease storage available by changing subscription to cloud storage service.
- Reduced upgrade costs – smaller local hard disk storage required as fewer files are stored locally.
- Security – improved security due to files being stored offsite, which keeps them safe from fire, flood, etc.
- Teleworking – makes it easier to work remotely as files can be saved to the cloud at an office and then accessed and worked on from home.
- Collaboration – cloud storage files can be shared with multiple users so that co-workers (e.g. Lloyd and his colleagues) can work together on the same files.

Limitations

- Downtime – if Lloyd's internet connection goes down he will not be able to access the files that are stored on the cloud.
- Heavy bandwidth use – constant saving and loading of large files (such as graphics) will make heavy use of network bandwidth, which could reduce network speeds and use up data allowances. Large data files may take long periods to sync before they can be worked on.
- Privacy – cloud storage files could potentially be accessed by a hacker and distributed without Lloyd's consent, or used for fraud.

Additional guidance

- Any reasonable response that relates the features and implications of cloud storage in the context of a games graphics artist is acceptable.
- Generic answers about cloud storage are not acceptable. **(10)**

2 (a) (1 mark for each identification and 1 additional mark for each appropriate expansion, up to a maximum of 2 marks each.)

- A touch screen (1) will allow users to choose menu options to pick their meal. (1)
- A barcode scanner (1) could be used to scan vouchers for discounts or loyalty cards; or to scan items chosen from a chiller cabinet. (1) **(4)**

(b) Provide a diagram of a user interface for a data entry screen, for a given data set.
(1 mark for inclusion of each of the following in the design, up to a maximum of 5 marks.)

- menu options for food choices
- menu option to go to payment screen
- at least one accessibility feature included (e.g. option to increase/decrease font size, 'listen to this page' feature)
- onscreen instructions/prompts/example data entry to help users
- button/navigation to move to next screen.

There is 1 additional mark for suitable layout/design showing all of the following: good use of layout and screen space. **(6)**

(c) Primary research will allow Harold to directly address what he wants to find out as he can target the exact audience that uses his fast food restaurants and ask them the exact questions he wants answered, whereas secondary sources would provide information about someone else's priorities.

- Primary data is likely to be far more recent and up-to-date than secondary sources, as he will carry out his data collection at the time he needs it.
- Harold will be able to gain more in-depth understanding of his customers as he can follow up answers by asking respondents further questions.
- The data collected may be more reliable than secondary sources as Harold can be sure of the methodology used to gather the information and put his own steps in place to prevent bias, etc.
- Harold can choose his own method of collecting data depending on the type of data he wants. For example, he can decide whether a questionnaire or one-to-one interviews will provide him with the most relevant and useful data, whereas he would have no control over the type of data available in secondary sources.

Additional guidance

- Any reasonable response that relates the benefits of primary data collection to the customer research that Harold wants to carry out is acceptable.
- Generic answers about primary data collection are not acceptable. **(10)**

3 (a) (1 mark for each identification and 1 additional mark for each appropriate expansion, up to a maximum of 2 marks each.)

- Virtual private networks (VPNs) create a secure connection over a public network such as the internet. (1) This will allow Aaliyah to connect to the drinks company's systems securely. (1)
- Remote desktop technologies allow users to access their computer from a different computer (1), so Aaliyah will be able to connect to her computer at the head office while she is at home. (1) **(4)**

(b) (1 mark for each identification and up to 2 additional marks for each appropriate expansion, up to a maximum of 3 marks each.)

- Mobile computing devices often have a mobile broadband connection (1), which allow users to access internet services wherever they are (1), so Aaliyah can use email, the web and even VoIP to keep in touch with the business while travelling. (1)
- Mobile computing devices have long battery life (1), which means they can be used for long periods of time without needing to be plugged in (1), so Aaliyah can continue to use the device even while travelling long distances without access to a plug socket. (1) **(6)**

(c) Provide an evaluation of the implications on Aaliyah's company when embarking on the launch of a social media presence. You should ensure you comment on which would be the most important. Your evaluation should be supported by relevant points which may include:

Employee and customer experience
- ease of use
- performance
- availability
- accessibility

Customer needs
- Is it what users want?
- Is it going to provide the 'right' information and experience?

Cost
- Is there a cost? One off or subscription?
- Enhancement costs for building a presence (for example, advertising, post promotion)?

Replacement or integration with current systems
- Does the social media presence integrate into an existing customer management system?
- How does the company robustly identify existing customers?

Productivity
- Is there a social media policy in place?
- How do you manage the personal use of social media?

Working practices
- Do employees have a policy to adhere to?
- How do you maintain a consistent and appropriate company image?

Security
- Is there any protection from attack by competitors/ enemies, and procedures in place to detect and manage?
- How do you ensure your presence isn't impacted by (or used to distribute) malware?(12)

4 (a) (1 mark for each identification and 1 additional mark for each appropriate expansion, up to a maximum of 2 marks each.)
- Privacy of users and their data is an ethical issue (1). If they permit data to be used (for example to target advertising) without their users consent, this could breach their privacy (1).
- Health and safety is an ethical issue when employees use IT systems in the workplace. (1) Organisations have an ethical duty to help prevent employees developing health problems such as RSI. (1)
- The accessibility of an organisation's IT systems is an ethical issue. (1) If appropriate assistive technologies are not in place, the IT systems may be inaccessible to employees with disabilities and therefore discriminatory. (1) **(6)**

(b) **File permissions and access levels**
- Users can be assigned different access levels to files, such as read-only, read/write and full control.
- These measures ensure a user cannot damage all data within the system as their access is limited.

Backup and recovery procedures
- These put in place clear steps for backing up data and recovering the data if it is damaged.
- These procedures ensure a business can recover quickly if a malicious user damages the IT system.

Passwords
- Using passwords to gain access to systems helps ensure that only authorised users who know the password can access them.
- Setting good complexity rules to passwords adds greater security by ensuring that passwords cannot be easily guessed.

Physical access control
- Techniques like locks and keys or biometrics to gain access to IT systems can prevent unauthorised users from physically gaining access to the systems.
- This helps prevent theft of and damage to systems.

Digital certificates
- These allow companies to transfer data securely over the internet using public key encryption.
- This means that they can use the HTTPS protocol for secure communication.
- Any data intercepted by a malicious user would not be readable. **(8)**

Firewall and Digital Security
- A firewall helps to prevent unauthorised access to the company network from the wider internet.
- It protects against hacking attempts and viruses.
- It can also protect devices inside the company from using unathorised services (for example BitTorrent).

(c) Provide an evaluation of the relevant legislation, stating if you think the decision is appropriate or not. Your evaluation should be supported by relevant points which may include some of the points below. You should ensure that your evaluation relates the legislation directly to the impact it may have on Haldrech Security.

Computer Misuse Act
- Protects against attacks on computer systems to gain unauthorised access and cause damage or theft to data, e.g. hacking, viruses.
- Anyone found in breach of this act is subject to unlimited fines and up to five years in jail.
- This helps deter any potential malicious users from attacking a business's systems.

Data Protection Act
- Protects the privacy of an individual's data being processed by anyone.
- Anyone found in breach of this act is liable to fines of up to £500, 000 as well as compensation to any individuals harmed by the breach.
- This act imposes significant costs on a business to ensure they have the right level of security to comply with legislation.
- However, it does improve consumer confidence in providing personal data for a business to use in their IT systems. **(12)**

For example, an answer might begin:
When considering the options available to Haldrech security to modernise their systems, they need to look at what protection is afforded them by current legislation as well as what demands that legislation places upon them. Whilst the Computer Misuse Act provides a deterrent for hackers and a means for punishment, the Data Protection Act places the onus on the provider of the computer system to ensure sufficient steps are taken in the first place to prevent intrusions.
You might then go on to discuss the specific requirements of the legislation in relation to security.

Unit 2: Revision task 1

Set task brief

Guided activities

1 Three tables (Support_request, Customer, Technician) create a robust database with a suitable user interface for technicians to enter support requests and to update support requests with resolutions of problems. Although "Resolved" does repeat, this is connected to the Support_request table identified.

2 Two data entry forms (Enter a support request, Update a support request).

3 (a) Two queries (All unresolved queries, All unresolved queries for a particular technician) plus three more queries behind the reports listed in part (b) – so five queries altogether.

(b) Three reports (Monthly summary report of requests dealt with by a particular technician, Monthly summary report of requests from a particular customer, Report of times taken by a particular technician to resolve queries).

4 You should have highlighted two items of repeating data:
- Customer, Customer address
- Technician allocated, Technician job title, Technician mobile no.

Activity 1: Entity relationship diagram

Guided activities

1 (a) Customer
(b) Technician allocated

2

Customer	Technician allocated
Customer address	Technician job title
	Technician mobile no.

3
- Customer address: Address, Town, Postcode
- Technician allocated: Technician first name, Technician surname

4
- Primary key for the Customer table is: Customer_ID (autonumber).
- Primary key for the Technician table is: Technician_ID (autonumber).

5

Request ID (primary key)
Reported by
Date/time reported
Problem description
Resolved?
Date/time resolved
Resolution description

6 (a) The **Customer** table is related to the **Support request** table by a one-to-many relationship.

(b) The **Technican** table is related to the **Suport_request** table by a one-to-many relationship.

7 Customer_ID and Technician_ID

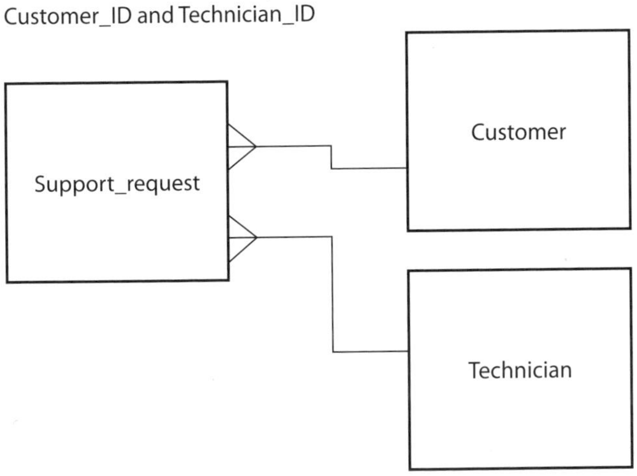

Activity 2: Data dictionary

Table Name:	Customer
Field name	**Attributes**
Customer_ID	Primary key, autonumber data type
Customer_name	Text data type, 25 characters, no validation
Address	Text data type, 25 characters, no validation
Town	Text data type, 25 characters, no validation
Postcode	Text data type, 8 characters, input mask to validate

Table Name:	Support_request
Field name	**Attributes**
Request_ID	Primary key, autonumber data type
Customer_ID	Foreign key linking to the Customer table. Integer data type
Technician_ID	Foreign key linking to the Technician table. Integer data type
Reported_by_first_name	Text data type, 25 characters, no validation
Reported_by_surname	Text data type, 25 characters, no validation
Date_time_reported	Date data type, default value of the current date/time, cannot be in the future.
Problem_description	Text data type, 150 characters, no validation
Resolved	Yes/No data type, default value of No
Date_time_resolved	Date data type, cannot be in the future
Resolution_description	Text data type, 150 characters, no validation

Note that you can set a default value for a field in the field properties. When used appropriately, default values help make the database easier to use as the user does not have to enter the data unless they want to change it.

Table Name:	Technician
Field name	**Attributes**
Technician_ID	Primary key, autonumber data type
Technician_f_name	Text data type, 25 characters, no validation
Technician_surname	Text data type, 25 characters, no validation
Title	Text data type, 20 characters, can only be Senior technician, Technician or Junior Technician
Mobile	Text data type, 12 characters, number only, no text characters

Activity 3: Design specification

Name and type	
Type: Form **Name:** Menu This form is not linked to any specific table, it just provides a menu to all the other database facilities. Each button links to the appropriate form, query or report.	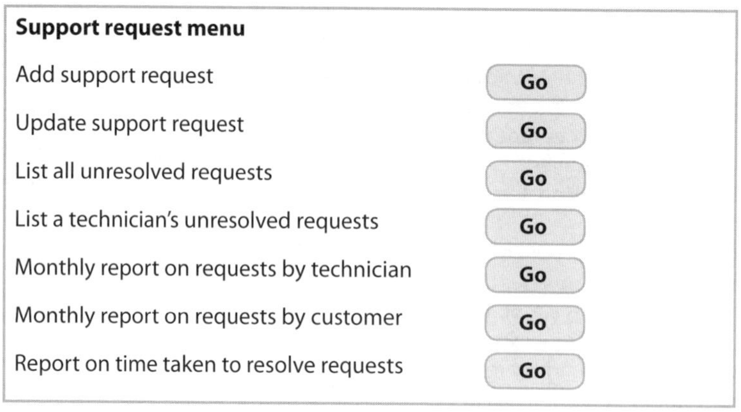
Type: Form **Name:** Add_Request This form allows input of a new support request. It is a data entry form. The customer name and technician allocated data is picked up off the Customer and Technician tables, and the primary key field for each is inserted in the Support_request table as a foreign key. The Save button saves the record, the Cancel button closes the form without saving the record.	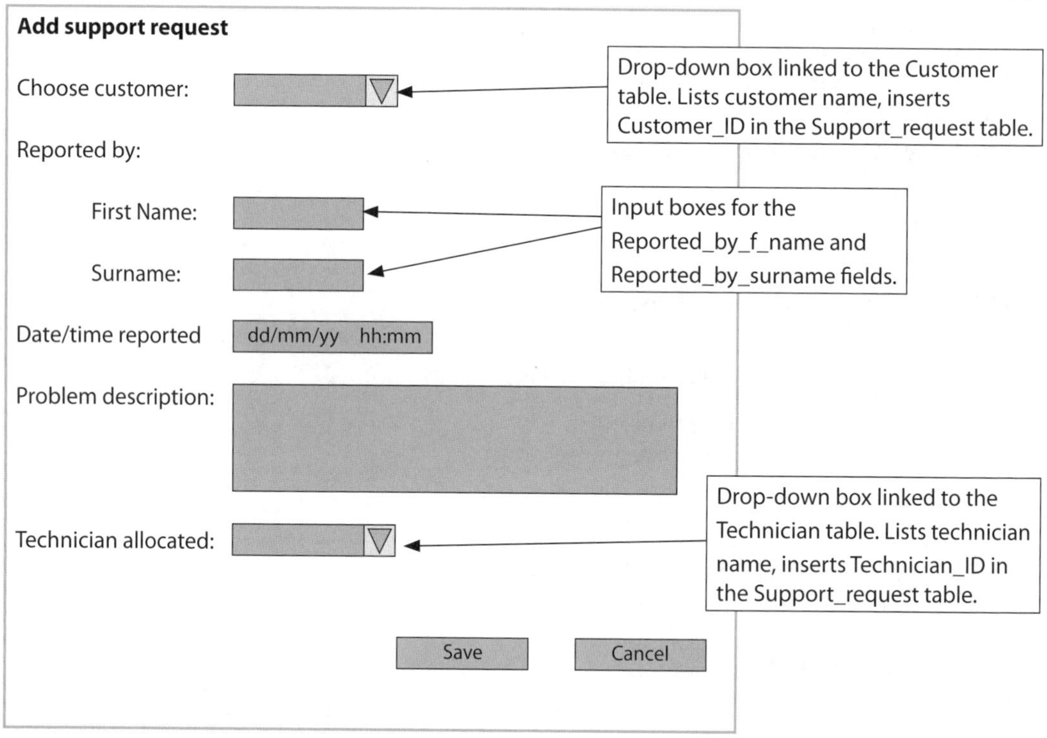
Type: Form **Name:** Update_ Support_request This form allows an update to be made on an existing support request. It is based on a query which uses the Request_ID (which the user enters as a parameter for the query) as a criterion and brings together the Customer, Technician and Support_ request tables.	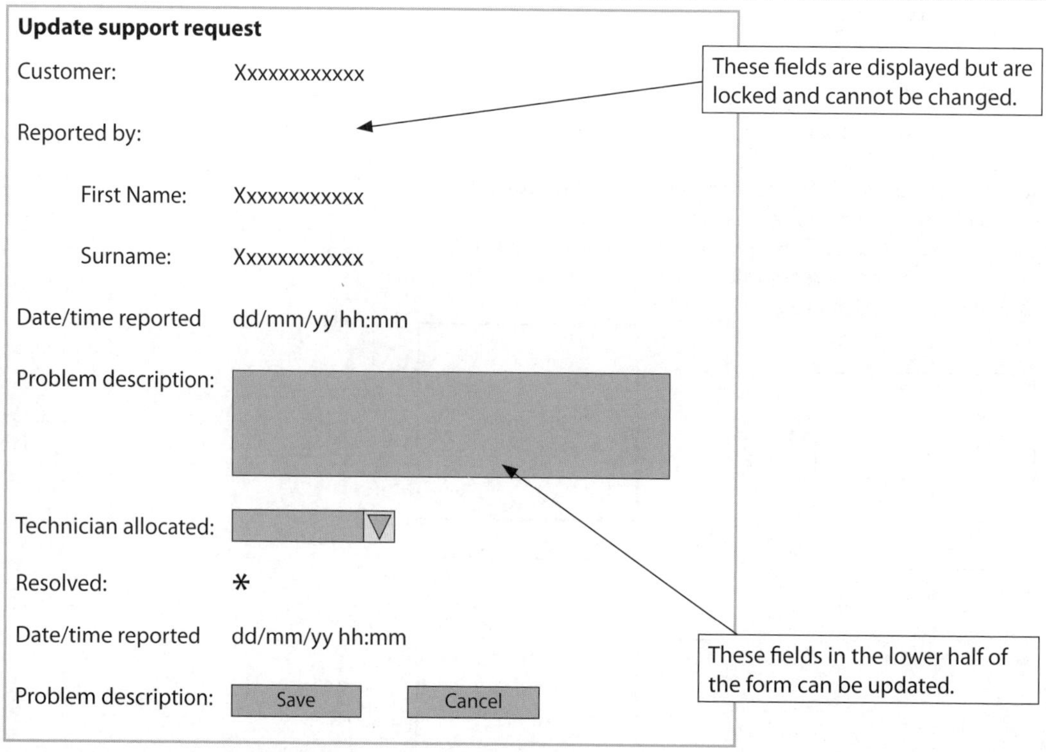

Type: Query
Name: List_all_unresolved_requests

This query lists all unresolved queries. It brings together the Support_request table and the Customer table so the customer name can be listed.

Table	Support_request	Support_request	Customer	Support_request	Support_request
Field	Request_ID	Customer_ID	Customer_name	Problem_description	Resolved
Criteria					No
Sort					

The criterion for the Resolved field is set to 'No' so only requests that have not been resolved are selected.

Type: Query
Name: List_a_technician's_unresolved_requests

Table	Support_request	Support_request	Support_request	Support_request	Technician	Technician	Support_request	Support_request
Field	Request_ID	Technican_ID	Customer_ID	Customer_name	Technician_surname	Technician_first_name	Problem_description	Resolved
Criteria					[Enter Technician Surname]			No
Sort								

This criterion will display a message box asking the user to enter the technician's surname, which will then be used to select only that technician's requests.

The criterion for the Resolved field is set to 'No' so only requests that have not been resolved are selected.

Type: Report
Name: Monthly report of support requests by technician

This report is based on a query which brings together the Technican, Customer and Support_request tables. The criterion for the query is the month required.
The report groups the output by technician, listing each request allocated to that technician in the month in question.

Support requests listed by Technician

Month: June 2016

Technician: Xxxxxxxxxx Xxxxxxxxx

Customer	Date/time reported	Problem	Resolved?
Xxxxxxxxx	dd/mm/yy hh:mm	Xxxxxxxxxxxxxxxxxxxxxxxx	X
Xxxxxxxxx	dd/mm/yy hh:mm	Xxxxxxxxxxxxxxxxxxxxxxxx	X
Xxxxxxxxx	dd/mm/yy hh:mm	Xxxxxxxxxxxxxxxxxxxxxxxx	X

Technician: nnnnnnn nnnnnnn

Customer	Date/time reported	Problem	Resolved?
Xxxxxxxxx	dd/mm/yy hh:mm	Xxxxxxxxxxxxxxxxxxxxxxxx	X

Type: Report
Name: Monthly report of support requests by customer

This report is based on a query which brings together the Technican, Customer and Support_request tables. The criterion for the query is the month required.
The report groups the output by customer, listing all the requests from the customer in the month in question.

Support requests listed by Customer

Month: June 2016

Customer: Xxxxxxxxxxx

Technician	Date/time reported	Problem	Resolved?
Xxxxxxxxx	dd/mm/yy hh:mm	Xxxxxxxxxxxxxxxxxxxxxxxx	X
Xxxxxxxxx	dd/mm/yy hh:mm	Xxxxxxxxxxxxxxxxxxxxxxxx	X
Xxxxxxxxx	dd/mm/yy hh:mm	Xxxxxxxxxxxxxxxxxxxxxxxx	X

Customer: Xxxxxxxxxxx

Technician	Date/time reported	Problem	Resolved?
Xxxxxxxxx	dd/mm/yy hh:mm	Xxxxxxxxxxxxxxxxxxxxxxxx	X

Type: Report
Name: Report on time taken to resolve requests

This report is based on a query which brings together the Technican, Customer and Support_request tables. The time to resolve the request is calculated in the query by subtracting the Date_time_reported field from the Date_time_resolved field.

Time taken to resolve requests

Request ID	Customer	Technician	Hours to resolve
nnnnnnn	Xxxxxxxxxxx	Xxxxxxxxxxxxx	hh
nnnnnnn	Xxxxxxxxxxx	Xxxxxxxxxxxxx	hh
nnnnnnn	Xxxxxxxxxxx	Xxxxxxxxxxxxx	hh
nnnnnnn	Xxxxxxxxxxx	Xxxxxxxxxxxx	hh

Note that when you carry out a calculation using fields with Date/Time data type, the answer will look a little odd as it is in days, so 19 hours would show as 0.78 days. You can use the DateDiff function in Access to display the result in hours.

Activity 4: Testing plan

Test Number	Purpose of test	Test data	Expected result	Actual result	Comments and action taken
Tests for fields in the Customer table					
1	Customer_name field	Joe Smith and Co	Accepted		
2	Address field	26 The Avenue	Accepted		
3	Town field	Bristol	Accepted		
4	Postcode field	a4bbx	Rejected		
5	Postcode field	BR99 1ZZ	Accepted		
Tests for fields in the Support_request table					
6	Customer_ID field referential integrity	9	Rejected (no Customer_ID 9)		
7	Customer_ID field referential integrity	4	Accepted		
8	Technician_ID field referential integrity	8	Rejected (no Technician_ID 8)		
9	Technician_ID field referential integrity	1	Accepted		
10	Reported_by_first_name	Alice	Accepted		
11	Reported_by_surname	Scott	Accepted		
12	Date_time_reported	30/12/2052 09:30:00	Rejected (in the future)		
13	Date_time_reported	32/13/16 28:30:00	Rejected (not a valid date)		
14	Date_time_reported	6/6/16 09:30:00	Accepted		
15	Problem_description	Mouse does not work	Accepted		
16	Resolved	Yes	Accepted		
17	Date_time_resolved	24/11/2032 10:30:00	Rejected (in the future)		
18	Date_time_resolved	9/14/16 08:45:00	Rejected (not a valid date)		
19	Date_time_resolved	5/6/16 10:30:00	Accepted		
20	Resolution_description	Replaced mouse	Accepted		
Tests for fields in the Technician table					
21	Technician_first_name	Winston	Accepted		
22	Technician_surname	Jamal	Accepted		
23	Title	Head Technician	Rejected		
24	Title	Junior Technican	Accepted		
25	Mobile	ABC123	Rejected		
26	Mobile	07222 33333	Accepted		

Activity 5: Database development and testing

Guided activities

1 My database development screenshots

The first task I completed was to create the **(a) tables**, using my data **(b) dictionary** as a guide.

I have added an **(c) input mask** for the Postcode field.

This is the **(d) Support_requests** table.

I have added a **(e) validation** rule with validation text for the Date_time_reported and **(f) Date_time_resolved** fields.

This is the **(g) Technician** table.

I have used a **(h) lookup** table to provide validation for the **(i) Title** field. The list contains three options: **(j) Senior** Technician, Technician and **(k) Junior** Technician.

2 **4** Follow the steps in the text import wizard.
2 From the External Data menu, choose Text file.

1 Create or open a database.

3 Find the file you need to import and choose to import it into a new table.

3 Importing data

The next task I completed was importing the sample **(a) data**. I used the Import Text **(b) Wizard**.

Once the data had been imported I used Append queries to split it up into the **(c) tables** I created before.

Once the data was imported, I checked the **(d) foreign** keys in the Support_requests table. I was then able to create the **(e) relationships** between the tables. Here are the **(f) relationships** I created.

4 Creating the objects

This is the Add support request **(a) form**.

This is a data **entry (b)** form. The user can select, the **(c) customer** and technician using **(d) drop-down** boxes which link to the Customer and Technician tables.

This is the **(e) Update support request**.form.

These are the **(f) queries** I created.

The design view of the **(g) query** for listing all unresolved requests looks like this.

This **(h) criterion** is set to 'No' so only requests which have not been **(i) resolved** are selected.

The **(j) output/result** of the query looks like this.

Here is the **(k) design** view of the query for listing a technician's unresolved support requests.

This **(l) criterion** will ask the user for the technician's **(m) surname**.

This is the result when the user enters the surname **(n) Platt** and the query is **(o) run**.

Next I completed my **(p) reports**.

This is the report for listing Support requests by **(q) technician**. To run the report the user enters the number of the **(r) month** that they want for the report.

This is the report for listing support requests by **(s) customer**. The user needs to enter the month number to **(t) run** this report.

This is the report for showing the **(u) time** taken to resolve support requests.

Once all the forms, reports and queries were complete, I created the **(v) menu** form, which has **(w) buttons** to access all the objects.

Database testing

Test Number	Purpose of test	Test data	Expected result	Actual result	Comments and action taken
Test for fields in the Customer table					
1	Customer field	Joe Smith and Co	Accepted	Accepted	
2	Address field	26 The Avenue	Accepted	Accepted	
3	Town field	Bristol	Accepted	Accepted	
4	Postcode field	a4bbx	Rejected	Rejected	The input mask converts the lower case characters to upper case automatically and will not allow a digit in the second character.
	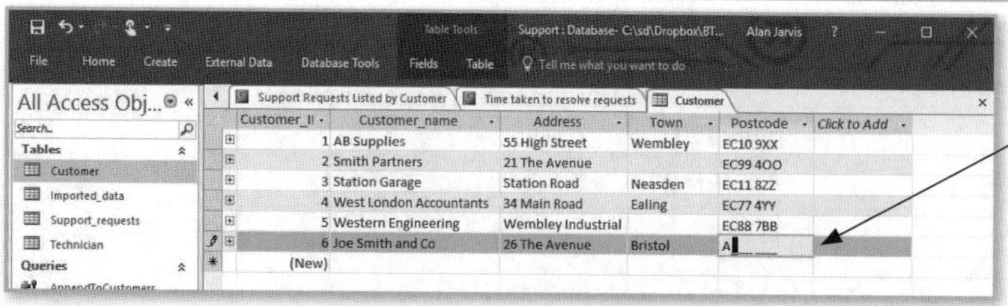				Here you can see the input mask working.
5	Postcode field in customer table	BR99 1ZZ	Accepted	Accepted	

Test for fields in the Support Request table					
6	Customer_ID field referential integrity	9	Rejected (no customer_ID 9)	Rejected	
	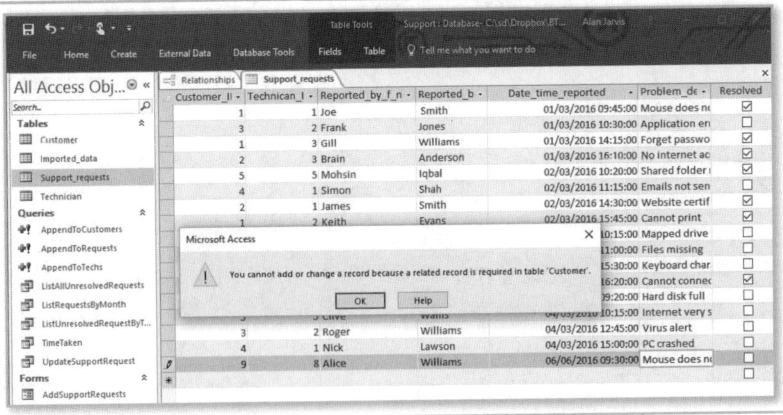				The referential integrity rules will not allow a Customer_ID to be entered which does not exist on the Customer table.
7	Customer_ID field referential integrity	4	Accepted	Accepted	
8	Technician_ID field referential integrity	8	Rejected (no Technician_ID 8)	Rejected	
	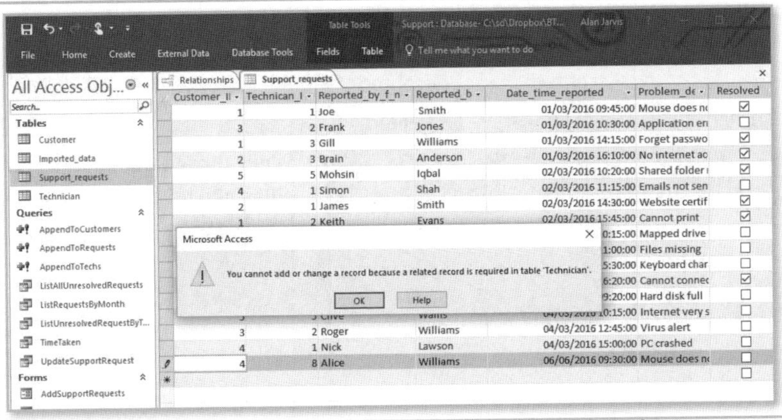				The referential integrity rules will not allow a Technician_ID to be entered which does not exist on the technician table.
9	Technician_ID field referential integrity	1	Accepted	Accepted	
10	Reported_by_first_ name	Alice	Accepted	Accepted	
11	Reported_by_ surname	Scott	Accepted	Accepted	
12	Date_time_reported	30/12/2052 09:30:00	Rejected (in the future)	Rejected	
	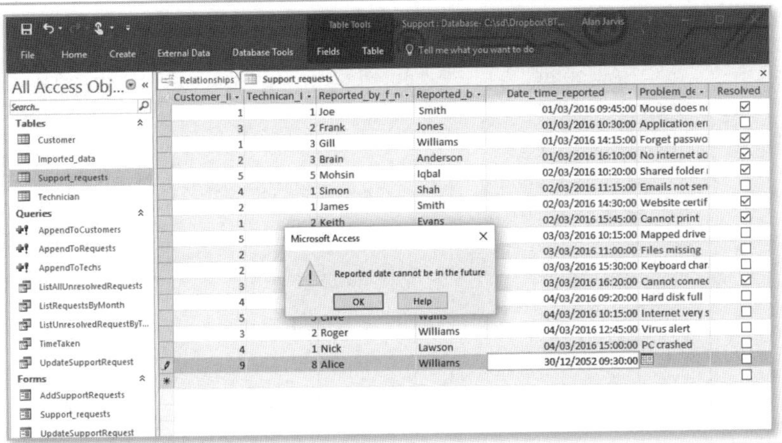				Future dates are rejected and the validation text appears in a message box.
13	Date_time_reported	32/13/16 28:30:00	Rejected (not a valid date)	Rejected	Standard Access error message for an invalid date
14	Date_time_reported	6/6/16 09:30:00	Accepted	Accepted	
15	Problem_description	Mouse does not work	Accepted	Accepted	
16	Resolved	Yes	Accepted	Accepted	

17	Date_time_resolved	24/11/2032 10:30:00	Rejected (in the future)	Rejected	
	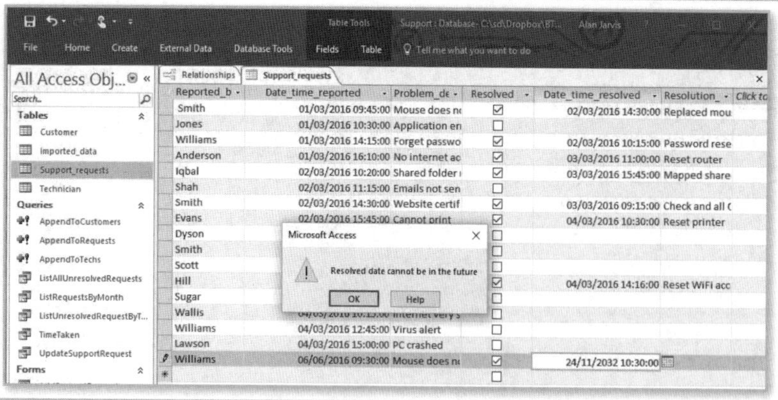				Future dates are rejected and the validation text appears in a message box.
18	Date_time_resolved	9/14/16 08:45:00	Rejected (not a valid date)	Rejected	Standard Access error message for an invalid date.
19	Date_time_resolved	5/6/16 10:30:00	Accepted	Accepted	
20	Resolution_description	Replaced mouse	Accepted	Accepted	
Test for fields in the Technician table					
21	Technician_first_name	Winston	Accepted	Accepted	
22	Technician_surname	Jamal	Accepted	Accepted	
23	Title	Head Technician	Rejected	Rejected	
	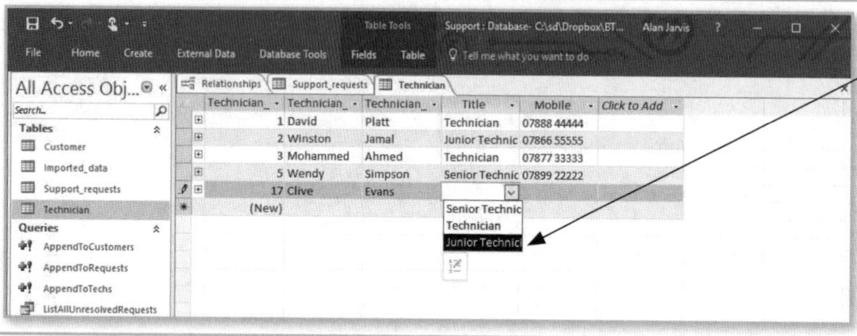				Only those values in the Lookup list are shown so other values cannot be selected.
24	Title	Junior Technician	Accepted	Accepted	
25	Mobile	ABC123	Rejected	Rejected	
	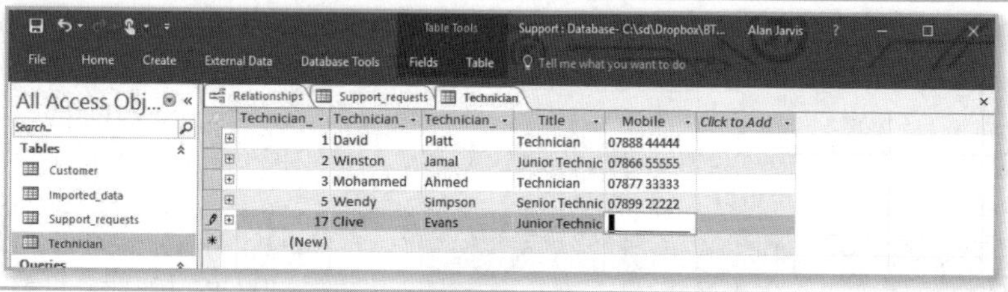				The input mask will only accept numbers so it is not possible to type letters.
26	Mobile	07222 33333	Accepted	Accepted	
Your evaluation					

Activity 6: Evaluation of your database solution

(a) **My database meets the needs of the brief in the following ways:**

The database I created has all the features listed in the Task Scenario and all the main features work as they should.

(b) **My database failed to meet the needs of the brief in the following ways:**

Although all the features work, there are a number of things that would need improving if this database was to be used for real.

(c) **During testing I discovered that:**

There were no errors in the tests I have done. This suggests that I have not tested the database thoroughly enough, and if I had more time I would create a more comprehensive test plan.

(d) **My database is easy to use because:**

Everything is labelled clearly and all the forms have Save and Cancel buttons. The layout for the forms is consistent (same colour scheme and fonts used) and fairly neat. The reports are also neat and consistent and clearly labelled.

(e) **I could improve the usability of my database in these ways:**

- Some of the labels on the forms still have the underscores for the field names (e.g. date_time_reported). These should be removed and the name made clear (e.g. Date and time reported).
- When the queries are run from the main menu there is no button to return to the menu, so it would be easier to use if the results of the queries where displayed in a form.
- On the Update support request form it would be better if, when you click the resolved check box, the date and time resolved field is automatically completed with the current date and time.
- When a user wants to update a support request, they need to know the request ID. To improve usability, it would be better if there were other ways to search for a support request, such as by company or person who reported it.

(f) **Elements of my database that work well are:**

The table structure and relationship links all work fine and the referential integrity options ensure, for example, that a support request record must relate to a record on the customer table. The use of drop-down combo boxes on the form makes the user select a valid customer for each request. I think the reports also work fine and do not need any improvement.

(g) **Elements of my database I could improve are:**

There is not really enough information on the database about the customer. For example, the name of the person at the company who reported the fault is recorded but not their contact details (email address, phone number, etc).

When reporting a new fault, the date and time reported should have the current date/time inserted automatically.

On the Update support request form the technician allocated is only shown by their ID number. It would be better if their name was shown.

The database should really have another table linked to the Support_request table that allows each update to an individual request to be recorded on a separate record. This would require a complete re-design of how supported requests are updated.

(h) **How well my database matches my designs:**

My design mostly matched the database I developed, although I had to change some minor layout features of the forms and reports as I went along. The designs of the ERD and data dictionary were correct and I did not need to modify them.

(i) **Some problems I encountered during development:**

I had a lot of difficulty getting the query behind the Time taken to resolve requests report to work. At first I just had the date of resolving the request subtracted from the date of reporting it. This gave me the number of days, when it would make much more sense to give the result as the hours. I spent some time trying to remember how to use a function to display just the hours, and eventually I got it to work.

(j) **In conclusion,**

I think my database does have all the required functions and they work fine. There is a lot more refinement I could do (as described above) if I had more time. I think the database might be OK as a prototype to get user opinions as to what else needs adding, but I don't think it would be very effective for use in real life because of the missing features I have listed. I think the database needs a lot more testing as I didn't really have time to test the forms and queries properly.

Unit 2: Revision task 2

Activity 1: Entity relationship diagram

Normalisation:

1NF involves splitting the repeating groups. These are the dogs and the competitions. Each needs a primary key:

- Primary key for the Dogs table is Dog_ID
- Primary key for the Competitions table is Competiton_ID.

The relationship between the two tables is many-to-many as one dog can be in many competitions and one competition can have many dogs entered.

This is not allowed, so I apply the rules of many-to-many relationships which is to create a link table, which I have called Competition_entries. This table:

- has a one-to-many relationship with the Dogs table, since one dog can have many competition entries
- has a one-to-many relationship with the competition table, since one competition can have many entries.

The primary key of this link table is Competition_entry_ID.

The Competition judge field in the raw data is not atomic – it needs breaking down into Judge_first_name and Judge_surname.

2NF: a composite key is not used so there is nothing to do at this stage.

3NF: there are no dependences for the non-key fields in any of the tables.

Here is the ERD

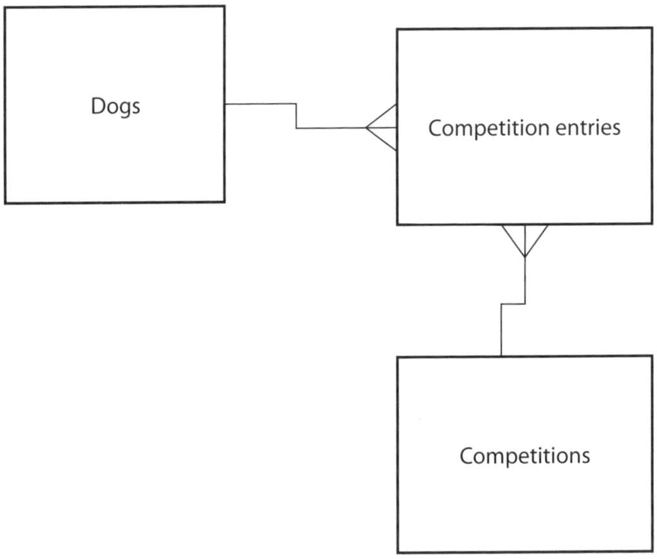

Activity 2: Data dictionary

Table Name:	**Dogs**
Field name	**Attributes**
Dog_ID	Primary key, autonumber data type
Dog_name	Text, 25 characters, no validation
Dog_breed	Text, 25 characters, no validation
Date_of_birth	Date, cannot be in the future
Owner_first_name	Text, 25 characters, no validation
Owner_surname	Text, 25 characters, no validation

Table Name:	**Competitions**
Field name	**Attributes**
Competition_ID	Primary key, autonumber data type
Competition_name	Text, 25 characters, no validation
Competition_time	Time, must be a valid time
Judge_first_name	Text, 25 characters, no validation
Judge_surname	Text, 25 characters, no validation
Winner	Text, 25 characters, must be a dog's name entered for this competition

Table Name:	**Competition_entries**
Field name	**Attributes**
Entry_ID	Primary key, autonumber data type
Dog_ID	Foreign key linking to the dogs table, integer data type
Competition_ID	Foreign key linking to the competition table, integer data type

Activity 3: Design the user interface

Name and type	
Type: Form **Name:** Menu This form is not linked to any specific table, it just provides a menu to all the other database facilities	**Byford dog show** Add new dog [Go] Add new competition entry [Go] Enter winning dog details [Go] List all dogs for a competition [Go] List competitions for a dog [Go] Breed entered for a competition [Go] All dogs born after 1/1/2013 [Go] Winning dog report [Go] Competition report [Go] Competition entries for a dog report [Go]

<table>
<tr><td>Type: Form
Name: Add_new_dog

This form allows input of a dog's details. It's a data entry form which is saved on the Dogs table.</td><td>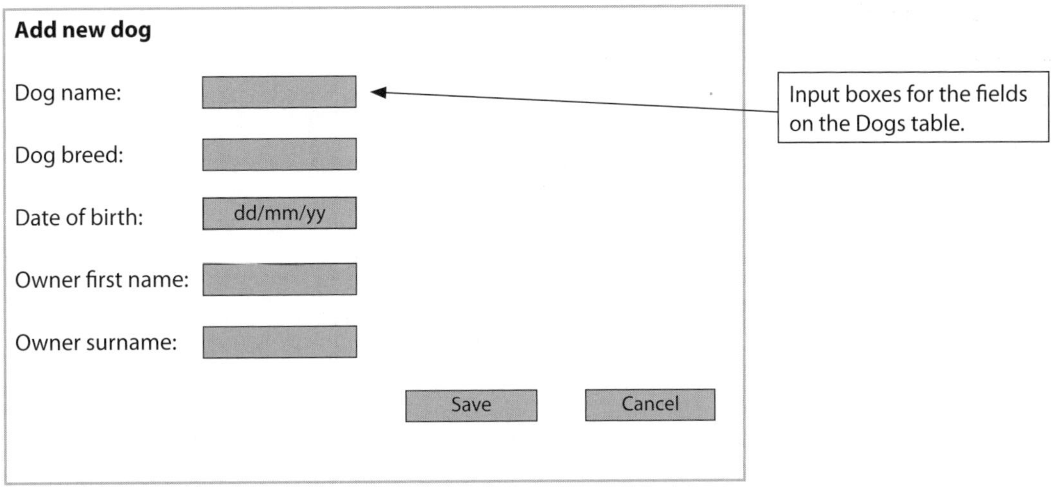
</td></tr>
<tr><td>Type: Form
Name: Add_competition_entry</td><td>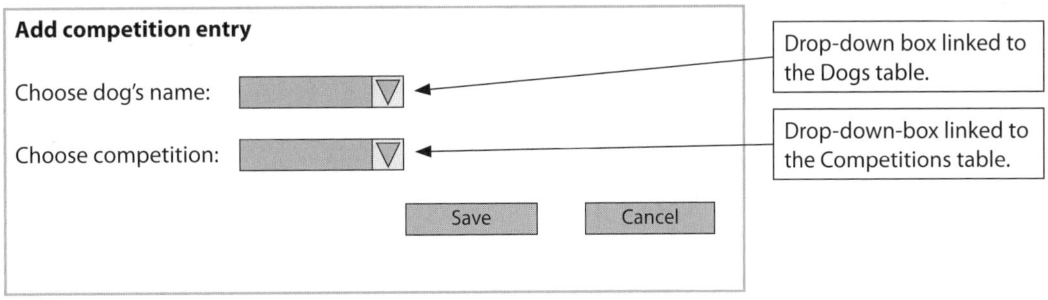
</td></tr>
<tr><td>Type: Form
Name: Choose_winner

This form has a drop-down box which lists the competitions from the Competitions table. The other drop-down box displays the results of a query which lists the dogs that were entered for the chosen competition. The user can then select the winner.</td><td>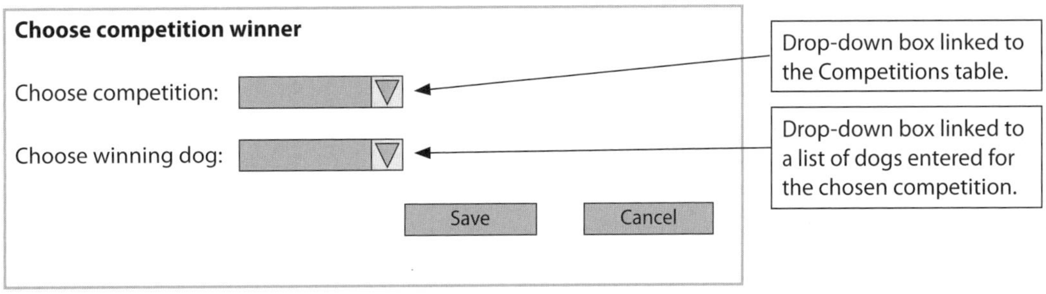
</td></tr>
</table>

Type: Query
Name: Dogs_entered_in_competition

Table	Competitions	Competitions	Competitions	Dogs	
Field	Competition_ID	Competition_name	Competition_time	Dog_name	
Criteria	[Enter competition ID]				
Sort					

Criteria here asks the user for the competition ID to use as a criterion to select the competition.

Type: Query
Name: Competitions_by_dog

Table	Dogs	Dogs	Dogs	Dogs	Competitions
Field	Dog_ID	Dog_name	Owner_first_name	Owner_surname	Competition_name
Criteria		[Enter dog name]			
Sort					

Criteria here asks the user for the dog name to use as a criterion to select the dog.

Type: Query
Name: Dogs_in_competition_by_breed

Table	Dogs	Competitions	Competitions	Dogs	
Field	Dog_Breed	Competition_ID	Competition_name	Dog_name	
Criteria	[Enter dog breed]	[Enter competiton ID]			
Sort					

Criteria firsts asks the user for the dog breed.

Then the competition ID.

Type: Query
Name: Young_dogs

Table	Dogs	Dogs	Dogs	Dogs	
Field	Dog_name	Date_of_birth	Owner_first_name	Owner_surname	
Criteria		>1/1/13			
Sort	Ascending				

This will sort the dogs alphabetically by their name.

This criterion will select only dogs with a date of birth after 1/1/13.

Type: Report
Name: Certificate
This shows the winning dog for a given competition in the format of a certificate.

Certificate

Congratulations to

Nnnnnnnn

Owned by: Xxxxxxxxxxxx

For winning the

Xxxxxxxxxxxxx

category

At Byford Dog Show 2016

Type: Report
Name: Entries_report

This lists the details (including dogs entered) of a given competition.
It uses a query to bring together the data from the Competition_entries table which identifies which dogs are entered in a competition. Other details are selected from the Dogs and Competitions tables. The query sorts the data by owner.

Entries report
Competition: Xxxxxxxxxxxx **Time: HH:MM**

Dog name	**Breed**	**Owner**
Xxxxxxxxxxxx Xxxxxxxxxxx	Xxxxxxxxxx	Xxxxxxxxxxx
Xxxxxxxxxxxx Xxxxxxxxxxx	Xxxxxxxxxx	Xxxxxxxxxxx
Xxxxxxxxxxxx Xxxxxxxxxxx	Xxxxxxxxxx	Xxxxxxxxxxx
Xxxxxxxxxxxx Xxxxxxxxxxx	Xxxxxxxxxx	Xxxxxxxxxxx

Type: Report
Name: Competitions_for_your_dog

Competitions for your dog
Dog: Xxxxxxxxxxxx
Owner: Xxxxxxxxxxx Xxxxxxxxxxx

Competition	**Time**	**Judge**
Xxxxxxxxxxxx Xxxxxxxxxxx	Xxxxxxxxxx	Xxxxxxxxxxx
Xxxxxxxxxxxx Xxxxxxxxxxx	Xxxxxxxxxx	Xxxxxxxxxxx
Xxxxxxxxxxxx Xxxxxxxxxxx	Xxxxxxxxxx	Xxxxxxxxxxx

Activity 4: Testing plan

Examples of possible tests

Test Number	Purpose of Test	Test Data	Expected result	Actual result	Comments and action taken
Tests for fields in the Dogs table					
1	Dog_name	Alfie	Accepted		
2	Dog_breed	Poodle	Accepted	Accepted	
3	Date_of_birth	10/9/2022	Rejected (in the future)	Rejected	
4	Date_of_birth	13/6/2012	Accepted	Accepted	
5	Owner_first_name	Shafina	Accepted	Accepted	
6	Owner_surname	Ahmed	Accepted	Accepted	
Tests for fields in the Competitions table					
7	Competition_name	Best looking dog	Accepted	Accepted	
8	Competition_time	56:97	Rejected (invalid time)	Rejected	
9	Competition_time	16:30	Accepted		
10	Judge_first_name	Bernard	Accepted		
11	Judge_surname	Irons	Accepted		
12	Winner	Shep	Rejected		Need to ensure this dog **is not** entered for this competition
13	Winner	Alfie	Accepted		Need to ensure this dog **is** entered for this competition
Tests for fields in Competitions_entries table					
14	Dog_ID	99	Rejected (no Dog_ID on the Dogs table)		
15	Dog_ID	1	Accepted		
16	Competition_ID	50	Rejected (no Competition_ID on the Competition table)		
17	Competition_ID	3	Accepted		

Activity 5: Develop and test the database – an example solution (any working solution is valid and may differ from that given here)

My database screenshots

The first task I completed was to create the tables, using my data dictionary as a guide.

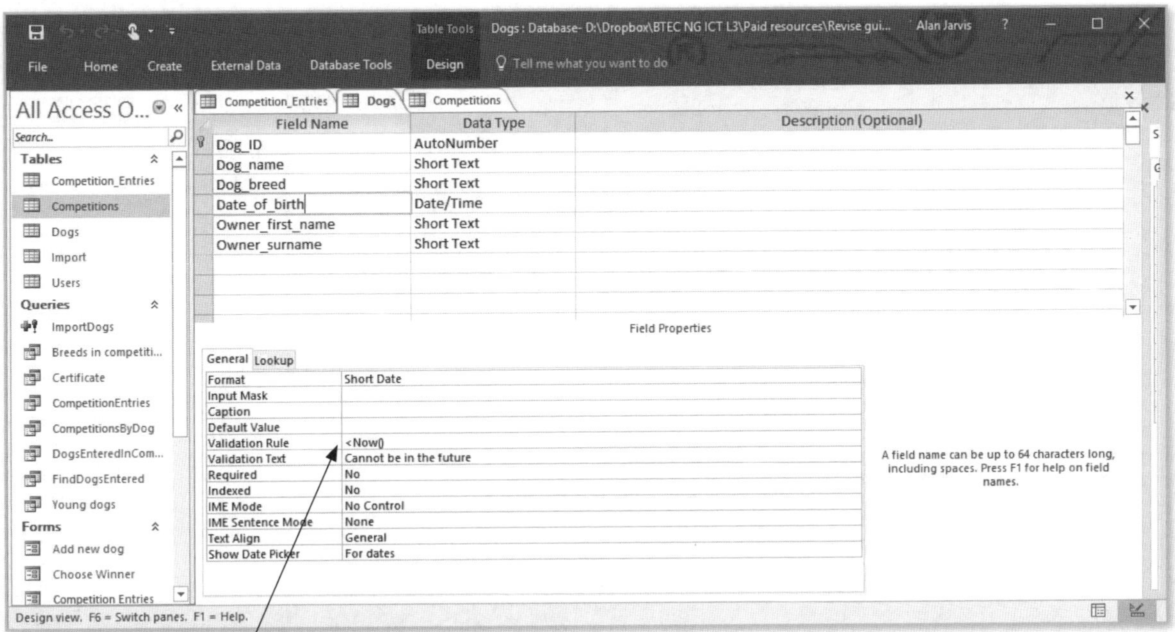

I added a validation rule for the date of birth.

This is the table design for the Competitions table.

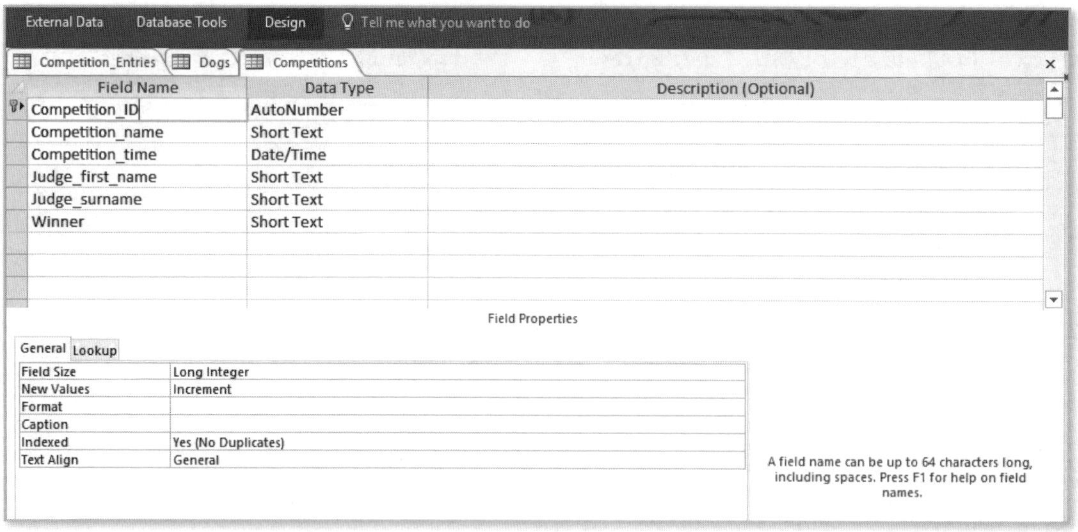

And this is the table design for the Competition_Entries table.

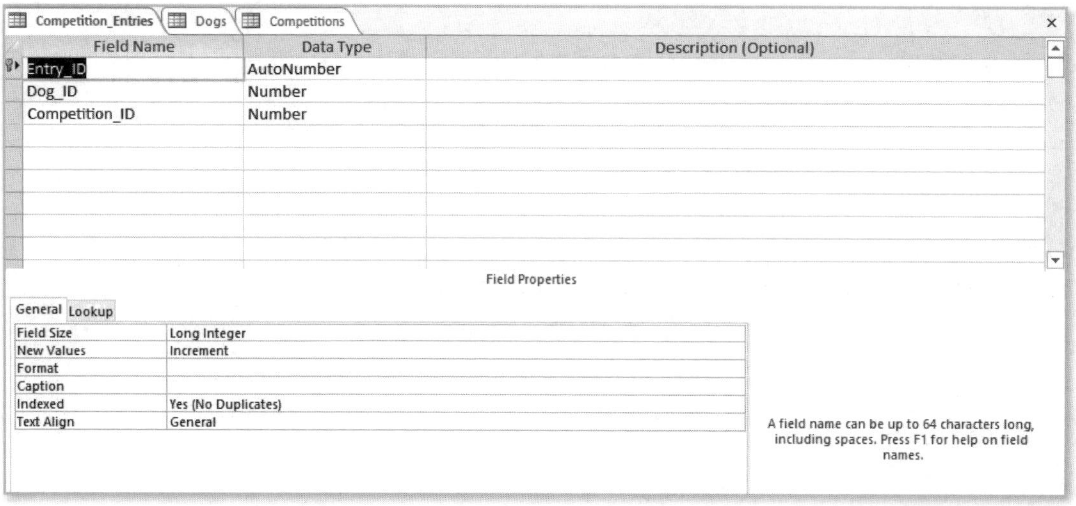

Then I imported the sample data using the text import wizard:

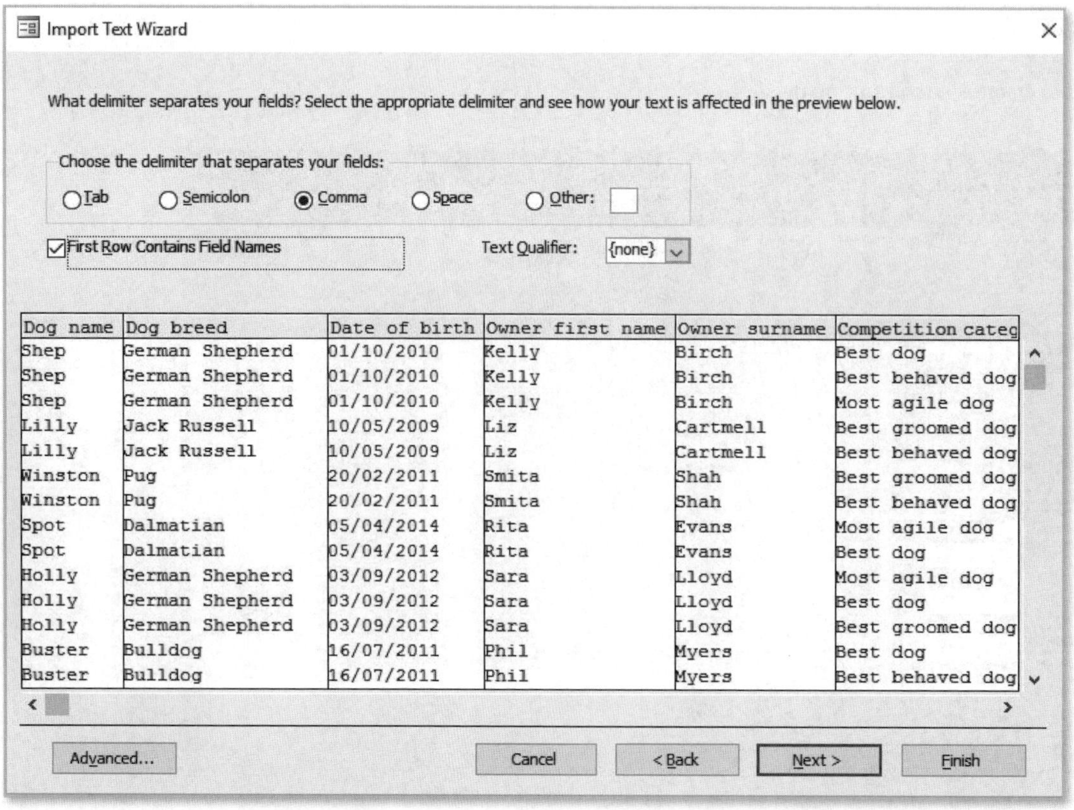

This is one of the steps of the text import wizard. Once the data had been imported I used Append queries to split it up into the tables I created before.

Here is the Append query I used to put records in the Dogs table:

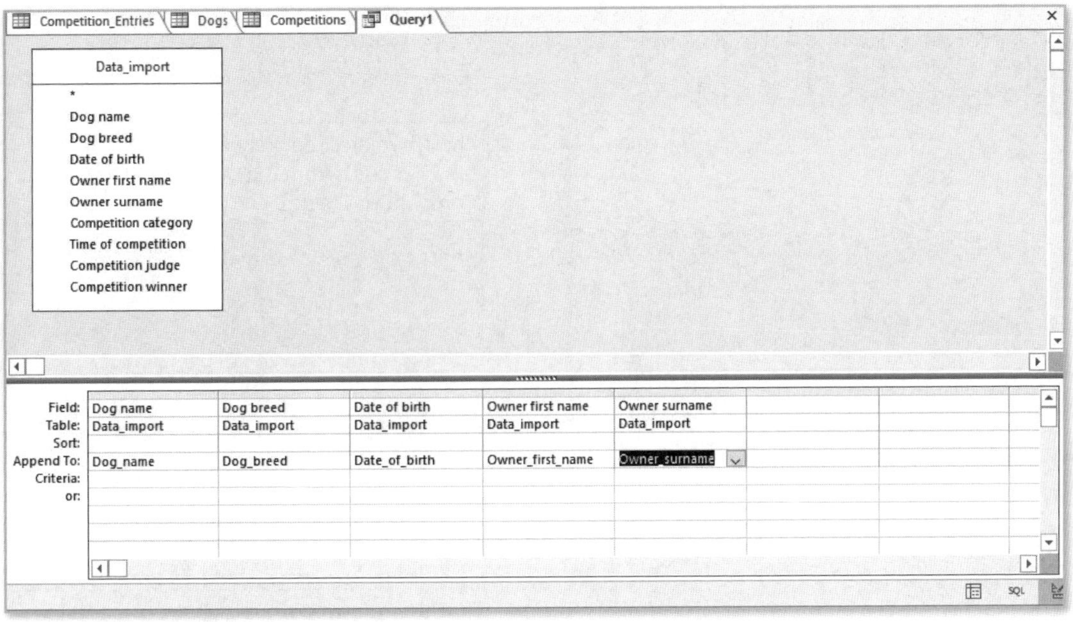

Once the data was imported and I checked the foreign keys in the Competition_Entries table,
I was then able to create the relationships between the tables. Here are the relationships I created.

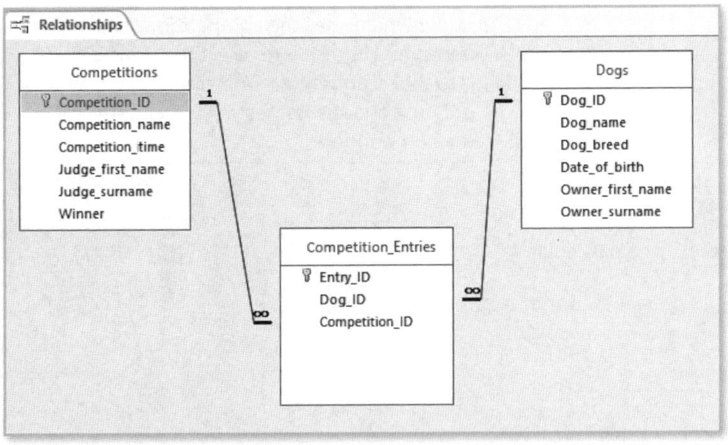

The next task was to create the forms.

This is the form I created to enter a new dog's details to the dogs table:

This form is used to add a dog to a competition. It inserts a record on the competition entries table:

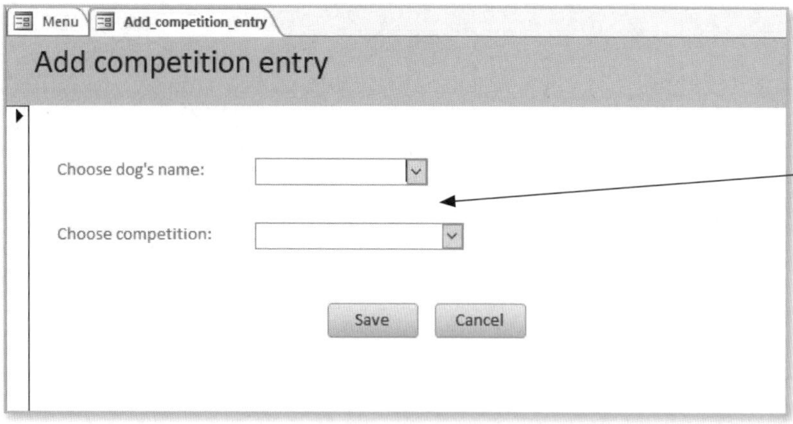

These two drop-down boxes pick up the records from the Dogs and Competitions tables.

Finally, this form is used to select the winner for a competition:

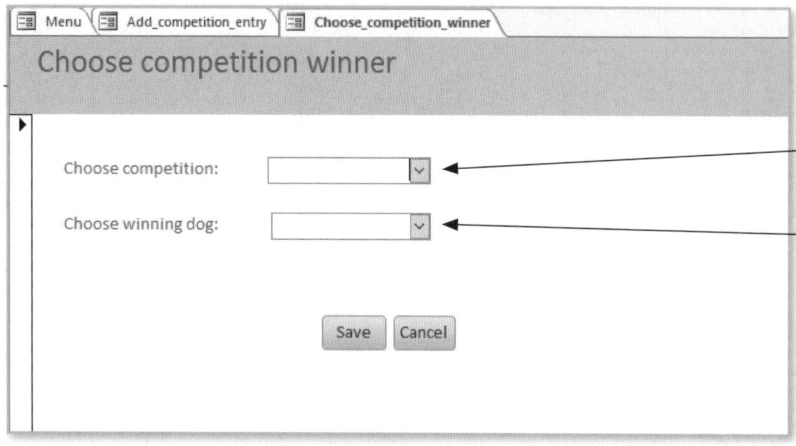

This drop-down box picks up the competition names from the Competitions table

This drop-down box collects its data from a query which uses the competition selected above as a criterion to select the dogs entered into that competition. This makes sure you can only select dogs' names who were entered for the competition.

Here are the queries I created. The first one selects all the dogs entered for a particular competition. This is the design view:

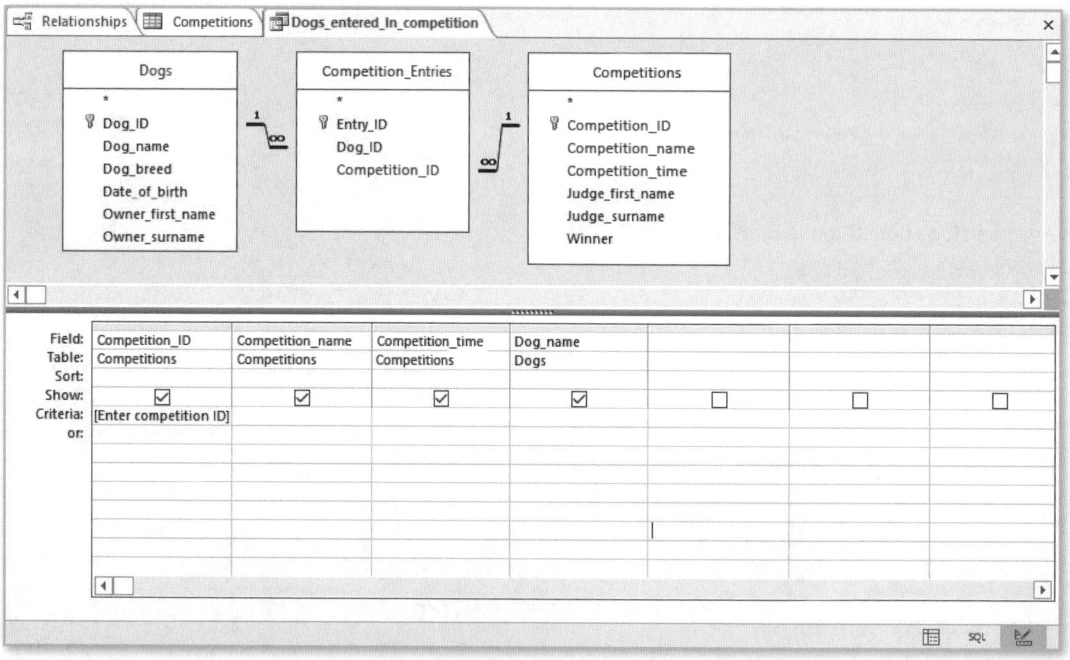

This is the output if competition number 1 is entered:

Competition	Competition_name	Competition_Time	Dog_name
1	Best dog	16:00	Shep
1	Best dog	16:00	Spot
1	Best dog	16:00	Holly
1	Best dog	16:00	Buster
1	Best dog	16:00	Honey
1	Best dog	16:00	Scruff
(New)			

The second one selects all the competitions a particular dog is entered for:

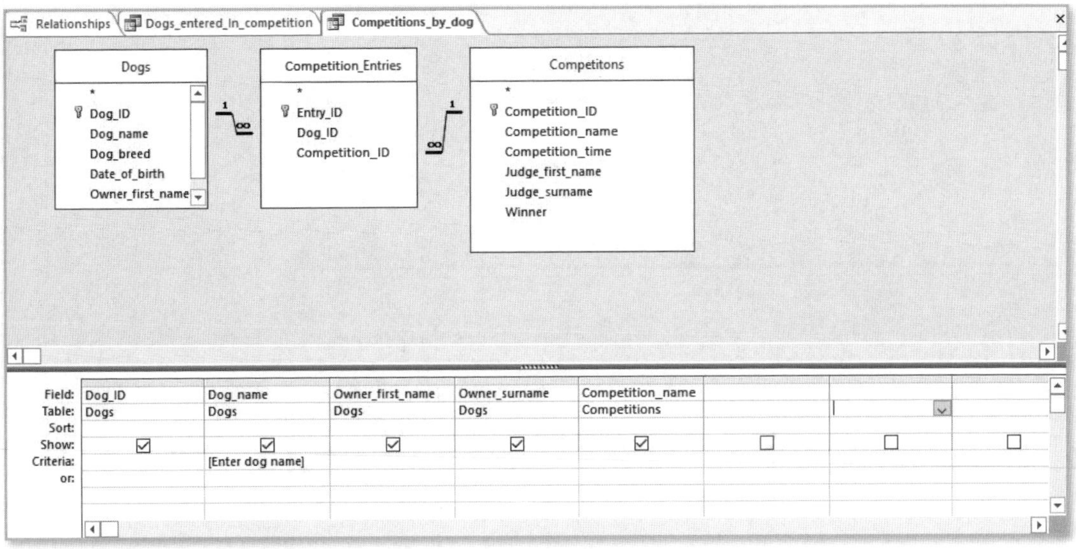

This is the output when the dog name 'Shep' is entered:

Dog_ID	Dog_name	Owner_first	Owner_surr	Competition_name
1	Shep	Kelly	Birch	Best dog
1	Shep	Kelly	Birch	Best behaved dog
1	Shep	Kelly	Birch	Most agile dog
1	Shep	Kelly	Birch	Best groomed dog
(New)				

This is the design view of the query that shows all the dogs of a given breed entered for a competition:

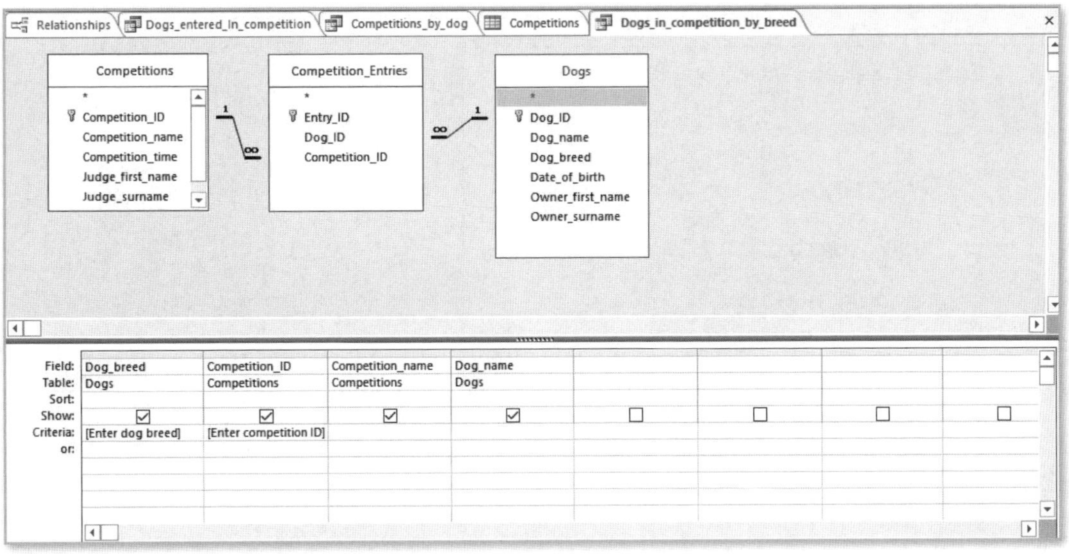

This is the query run with the breed 'Pug' and competition ID 1 entered:

Dog_breed	Competition	Competition_name	Dog_name	Competition_Time
Pug	2	Best behaved dog	Winston	14:00
	(New)			

The final query lists all dogs born after 1/1/2013. This is the design view:

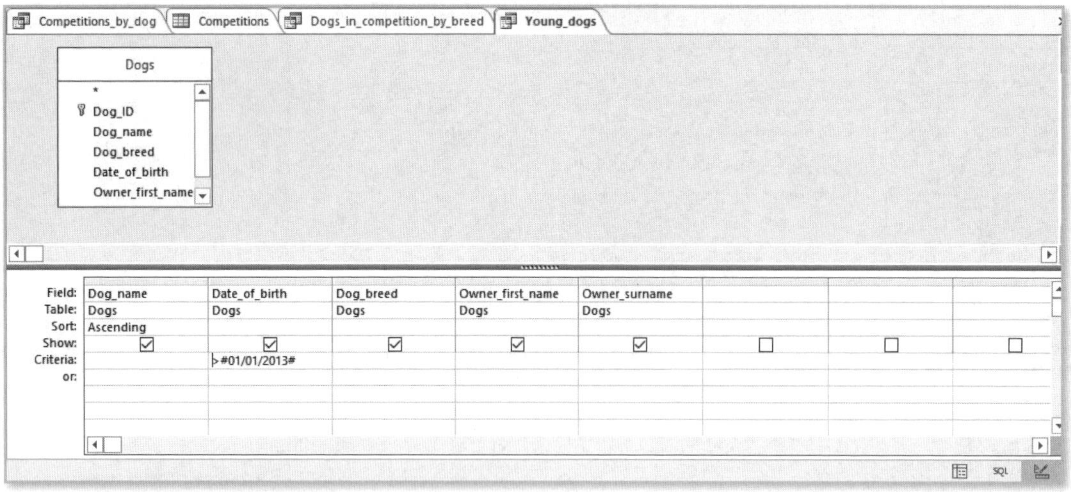

And this is the query running:

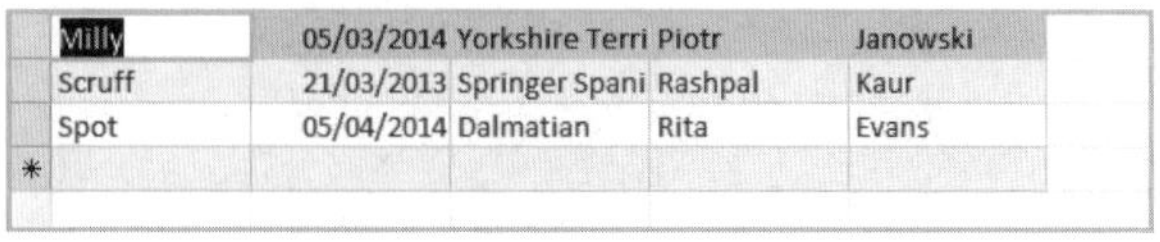

Milly	05/03/2014	Yorkshire Terri	Piotr	Janowski
Scruff	21/03/2013	Springer Spani	Rashpal	Kaur
Spot	05/04/2014	Dalmatian	Rita	Evans
*				

These are the reports that I created:
Here is the certificate for the winning dog. The query that provides the data for this report asks you for the competition number. This is the certificate for competition 1:

This is the report of all the dogs entered for the competition number entered by the user, sorted by owner surname:

Entries report

Competition:	Best behaved dog	Time:	14:00

Dog name	Breed	Owner	
Shep	German Shepherc	Kelly	Birch
Lilly	Jack Russell	Liz	Cartmell
Sandy	Whippet	Kieran	Hales
Honey	Beagle	Ruth	Hamilton
Milly	Yorkshire Terrier	Piotr	Janowski
Buster	Bulldog	Phil	Myers
Winston	Pug	Smita	Shah
Frisky	Collie	Nicki	Spencer

03 August 2016 Page 1 of 1

This is the report which lists all the competitions for a given dog (whose name is entered by the user):

Competitions for your dog

Dog's name: Shep

Owner: Kelly Birch

Competition	Time	*Judge*	
Best behaved dog	14:00	Simon	Jones
Best groomed dog	15:00	Anita	Patel
Most agile dog	15:30	Eric	Smith
Best dog	16:00	Alice	Wilson

03 August 2016 Page 1 of 1

Once I had developed all the forms, queries and reports, I created the main menu:

Byford Dog Show

Add new dog	Go
Add new competition entry	Go
Enter winning dog details	Go
List all dogs for a competition	Go
List competitions for a dog	Go
Winning dog report	Go
Breed entered for a competition	Go
All dogs born after 1/1/2013	Go
Competition report	Go
Competition entries for a dog report	Go

Testing results

Test Number	Purpose of Test	Test Data	Expected result	Actual result	Comments and action taken
1	Dog_name in Dogs table	Alfie	Accepted	Accepted	
2	Dog_breed in Dogs table	Poodle	Accepted	Accepted	
3	Date_of_birth in Dogs table	10/9/2022	Rejected (in the future)	Rejected	

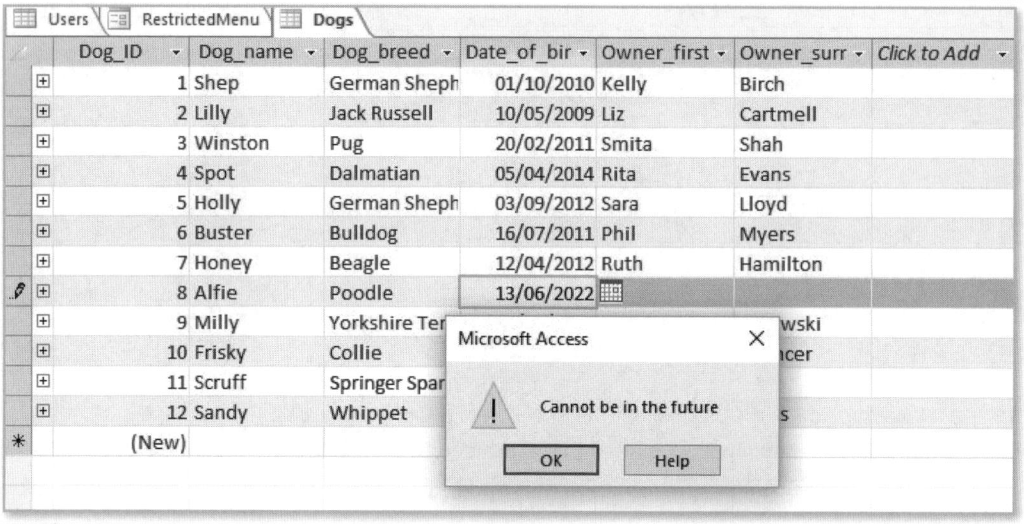

Dog_ID	Dog_name	Dog_breed	Date_of_bir	Owner_first	Owner_surr	Click to Add
1	Shep	German Sheph	01/10/2010	Kelly	Birch	
2	Lilly	Jack Russell	10/05/2009	Liz	Cartmell	
3	Winston	Pug	20/02/2011	Smita	Shah	
4	Spot	Dalmatian	05/04/2014	Rita	Evans	
5	Holly	German Sheph	03/09/2012	Sara	Lloyd	
6	Buster	Bulldog	16/07/2011	Phil	Myers	
7	Honey	Beagle	12/04/2012	Ruth	Hamilton	
8	Alfie	Poodle	13/06/2022			
9	Milly	Yorkshire Ter			wski	
10	Frisky	Collie			ncer	
11	Scruff	Springer Spar				
12	Sandy	Whippet			s	
(New)						

Test Number	Purpose of Test	Test Data	Expected result	Actual result	Comments and action taken
4	Date_of_birth in Dogs table	13/6/2012	Accepted	Accepted	
5	Owner_first_name in Dogs table	Shafina	Accepted	Accepted	
6	Owner_surname field in Dogs table	Ahmed	Accepted	Accepted	
Tests for the Competitions table					
7	Competition_name	Best looking dog	Accepted	Accepted	
8	Competition_time	56:97	Rejected (invalid time)	Rejected	

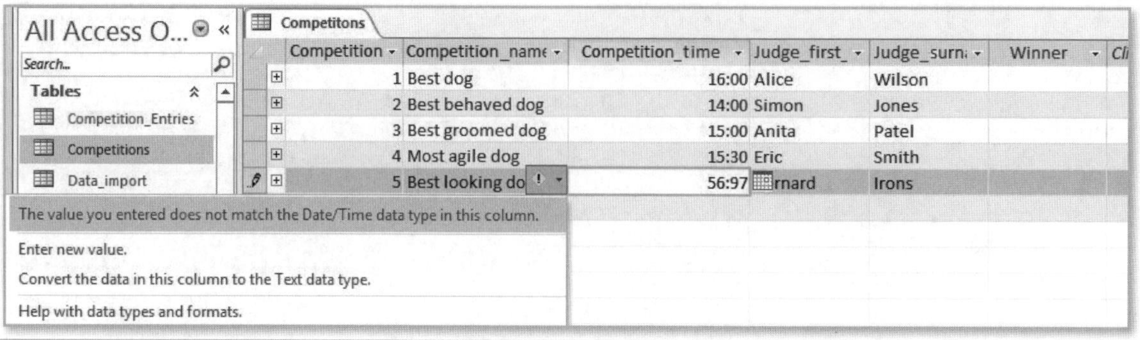

Competition	Competition_name	Competition_time	Judge_first_	Judge_surn	Winner	Cli
1	Best dog	16:00	Alice	Wilson		
2	Best behaved dog	14:00	Simon	Jones		
3	Best groomed dog	15:00	Anita	Patel		
4	Most agile dog	15:30	Eric	Smith		
5	Best looking do	56:97	rnard	Irons		

Test Number	Purpose of Test	Test Data	Expected result	Actual result	Comments and action taken
9	Competition_time	16:30	Accepted	Accepted	
10	Judge_first_name	Bernard	Accepted	Accepted	
11	Judge_surname	Irons	Accepted	Accepted	
12	Winner	Shep	Rejected	Rejected	Need to ensure this dog **is not** entered for this competition.

					As long as you use the form, you can only see dogs who are entered for the competition.
13	Winner	Alfie	Accepted		Need to ensure this dog **is** entered for this competition.
Tests for Competitions_entries table					
14	Dog_ID	99	Rejected (no Dog_ID on the Dogs table)		
	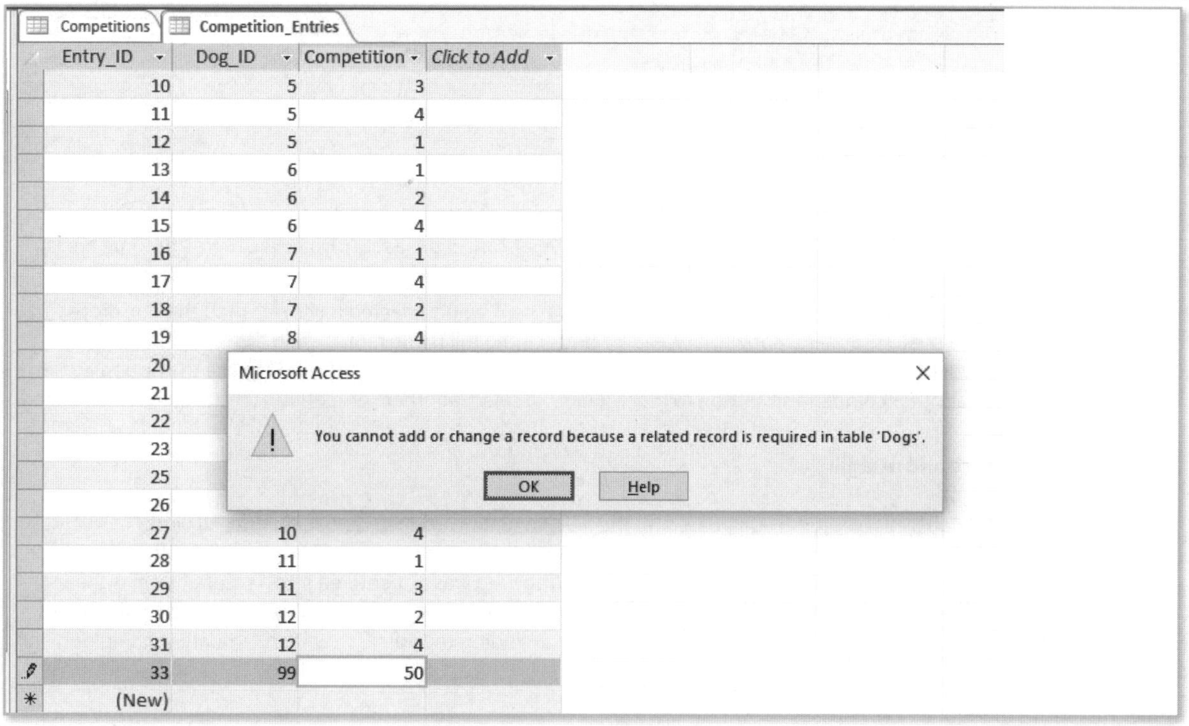				
15	Dog_ID	1	Accepted		
16	Competition_ID	50	Rejected (no Competition_ID on the Competition table)		

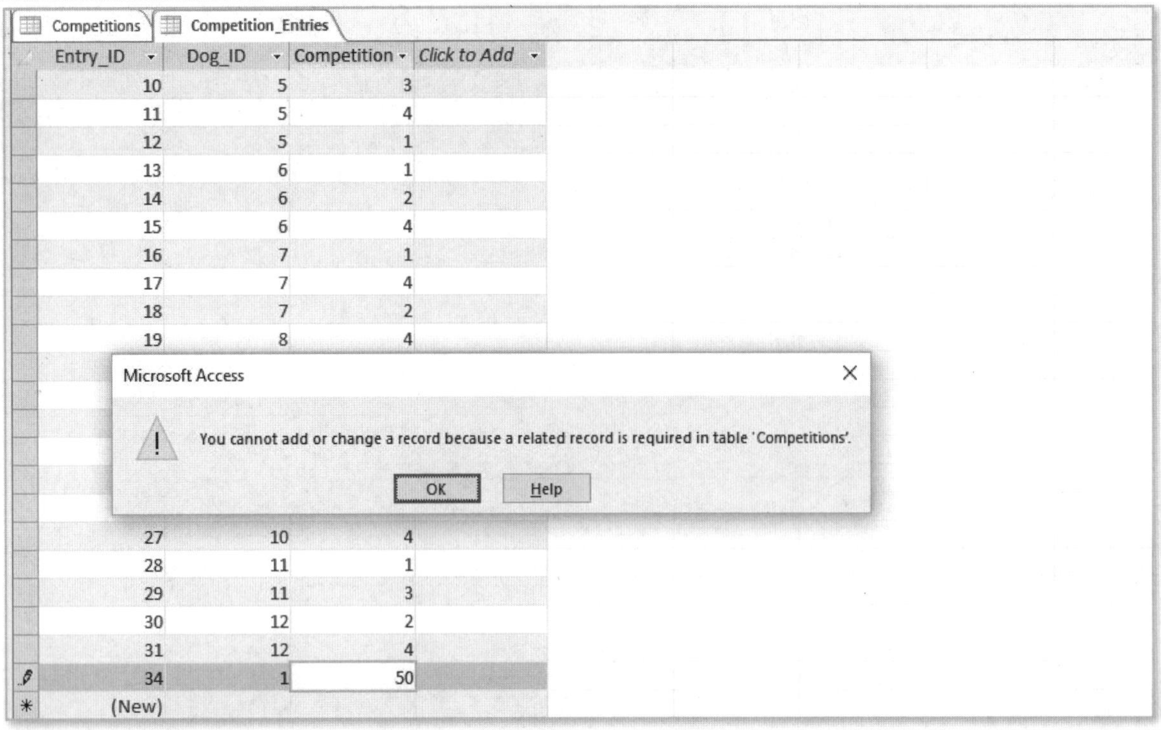

Entry_ID	Dog_ID	Competition	Click to Add
10	5	3	
11	5	4	
12	5	1	
13	6	1	
14	6	2	
15	6	4	
16	7	1	
17	7	4	
18	7	2	
19	8	4	
27	10	4	
28	11	1	
29	11	3	
30	12	2	
31	12	4	
34	1	50	
(New)			

17	Competition_ID	3	Accepted	Accepted	

Activity 6: Evaluation of your database solution

How well does my solution meet the requirements of the scenario?

I think my database does a reasonable job of meeting the requirements but there are some areas that need improvement.
My database has consistent menus and forms that are clear and have buttons to save or cancel the action. However, there are some areas where the interface could be made easier to use:

- When making a selection from the drop-down boxes, although the full text of the item being selected is shown when the box drops down, once the selection is made only the ID number is shown. It would be better if the full name remained in the drop-down box.
- Entering dogs into competitions is tedious because for each entry you have to go back to the main menu and choose the option again. It would be better if there was an 'Add another competition' button to make it easy to select another competition for the currently selected dog.

Evaluation of the quality, performance and usability of the database

I have carried out some testing of the database tables for my database and the field validation and referential integrity all works correctly. However, the way the database is set up allows a user to edit the tables directly rather than using the forms. This means that they could create problems, like entering the same dog for a competition twice or selecting a dog who was not entered into a competition as the winner. The database really needs a separate user interface (perhaps web-based) where the user cannot directly edit the data in the tables. This type of user interface would also need to provide a complete range of options, including the ability to edit and update existing dog and competition entries.

There are some usability issues, as mentioned previously.

Evaluation of the changes made during the development and testing process

The design I created was correct so I didn't need to make many changes during development, just add a few things I forgot. The testing revealed a few limitations of the system, such as those mentioned above. For example, in the table validation there is no way to prevent users entering the same dog twice into a competition, and the form does not prevent doing this either. The way to correct the form would be to use a query to select dogs which were not already in the selected competition. This query would then provide the list for the dog name drop-down box. I did not have time to implement this.

Conclusion

I think the database I have designed and created meets some of the requirements of the user, but there is quite a lot which would need to be added or improved to make the database really useful and overcome some of the problems I have described. The designs I created for the tables, ERD and data dictionary were correct. The testing plan was adequate for the tables but the forms, queries and report also need testing.